"This book is a breakthrough. Simple, powerful, and ready to help anyone who's ready. Profound wisdom, generously offered."

—SETH GODIN, author of *The Song of Significance*

"I've been a fan of Lodro's books and in-person meditations for many years. With warmth and humor, he has a practical and encouraging way of reminding us that we are good enough and that the consistent practice of being present can have a profound impact on our lives. Lodro's writing makes these big ideas feel accessible, totally doable, and fun! This book feels like a big exhale and a reminder we all need."

—KRYSTEN RITTER, actress and national best-selling author of *Retreat* and *Bonfire*

"Lodro Rinzler invites us to rediscover 'basic goodness' as the ground of our lives, relationships, and society, moving from self-acceptance to compassion for others, and finally to transforming how we see the world. This book beautifully blends Buddhist wisdom with down-to-earth guidance. With practical reflections and everyday practices, it shows how to work with doubt, shame, and conflict, and how to recognize the innate goodness in yourself, your loved ones, strangers, and even the world at large. Timely, relevant, and useful for this modern world, it is a guide to living with clarity, confidence, and kindness—just right here, right now."

—DZA KILUNG RINPOCHE, author of *The Free Mind*

"If you ever need a pep talk and a reminder that life is basically good—this is the book for you!"

—ALAN CUMMING, actor and director

"Lodro Rinzler's new book, *You Are Good, You Are Enough,* is timely and deeply needed in today's world. It offers guidance for healing from within—wisdom that he not only teaches but also lives by. Having shared these insights for many years, Lodro's dedication to helping younger generations of contemplative-minded people reconnect with their own basic goodness is truly inspiring. His care and outreach reflect his genuine altruism and compassionate heart. In an age of confusion and competition that so often leads to hopelessness, his message—that we are good enough as we are—brings us both clarity and hope."

—DZIGAR KONGTRUL RINPOCHE,
author of *Training in Tenderness*

You Are Good You Are Enough

Free Yourself from the Trap of Doubt and Return to Basic Goodness

LODRO RINZLER

SHAMBHALA

Shambhala Publications, Inc.
2129 13th Street
Boulder, Colorado 80302
www.shambhala.com

Cover art: Andrew Krasovitckii / Shutterstock
Cover design: Daniel Urban-Brown
Interior design: Meredith Jarrett

9 8 7 6 5 4 3 2 1

First Edition
Printed in the United States of America

Shambhala Publications makes every effort to print on acid-free, recycled paper. Shambhala Publications is distributed worldwide by Penguin Random House, Inc., and its subsidiaries.

Library of Congress Cataloging-in-Publication Data
Names: Rinzler, Lodro author
Title: You are good, you are enough: free yourself from the trap of doubt and return to basic goodness / Lodro Rinzler.
Description: First edition. | Boulder, Colorado: Shambhala, [2026] | Includes bibliographical references. |
Identifiers: LCCN 2025012759 | ISBN 9781645474166 trade paperback
Subjects: LCSH: Spiritual life—Buddhism | Meditation—Buddhism | Good and evil—Religious aspects—Buddhism
Classification: LCC BQ5660 .R564 2026 | DDC 294.3/444—dc23/eng/20250827
LC record available at https://lccn.loc.gov/2025012759

The authorized representative in the EU for product safety and compliance is eucomply OÜ, Pärnu mnt 139b-14, 11317 Tallinn, Estonia, hello@eucompliancepartner.com.

For Ruby—may you always know, without doubt,
the beauty and goodness that lives within you.

CONTENTS

PART ONE

YOU ARE BASICALLY GOOD

1 THE GOLDEN BUDDHA

Let's begin with a big idea, one that your parents, your schooling, and society as a whole may have kept from you: You're okay just as you are. You don't need fixing. At your core, you are basically good.

There's a story from Thailand that captures this beautifully. In the mid-twentieth century, monastics were moving a large clay Buddha statue. During the move the statue fell, cracking open in places. When the monks examined the cracks, they were stunned to see a glimmer of something beneath the clay. They carefully chipped away at the clay, revealing a solid-gold Buddha underneath.

Centuries earlier, to protect the statue from invading tribes, it had been covered in clay to disguise its value. Over time, the true nature of the statue was forgotten until this incident revealed it. Today people from all over the world visit Thailand to see the statue that happened to be gold all along.

We're very much like this statue. We may feel like we're covered in layers of flaws or imperfections. Many of us are taught, implicitly or explicitly, that we're not enough as we are. As a result, we begin searching outside ourselves for happiness and contentment, covering our true golden nature with layers of doubt and insecurity.

Let's face it, many of us struggle to feel content. Instead of being satisfied with our lives, we often believe we're missing something. We think we *should* want more. Maybe your home is nice, but wouldn't it be nicer with an extra bedroom? Maybe you're enjoying your job, but wouldn't a promotion and a raise make you happier? You're content with the person you're dating, but isn't it time they take the next step?

This constant reaching and grasping for more is like scratching an itch that never goes away. When we get what we want, we want something else. When we don't get what we want, we fall into a scarcity mindset, feeling unfulfilled and disappointed. If you picked up this book, I am guessing this sounds familiar.

It's not just you; it's everyone. This is the very nature of suffering as the Buddha described 2,600 years ago. It's that we have somehow distanced ourselves from our true, peaceful state and are chasing down all the wrong alleys to try to reclaim it. Instead of realizing the gold within, we continue to cover ourselves in mud and dirt. The thing the Buddha taught that is still making waves today is that we are not broken and in need of fixing. We are inherently good.

Let's talk about this term "basic goodness." In a world where "basic" has become shorthand for unremarkable or uncool, let's reclaim it. Here, "basic" refers to something essential and fundamental, a core part of who you are. Basic goodness is not something you need to acquire; it's already within you. You could also think of it as fundamental, primordial, foundational, and inherent. In other words, we're saying let's strip away some of the mud and clay that's not been helpful for you and go back to basics—who you fundamentally are underneath.

As for the other half of the term, "good" here does not mean better than others. It doesn't mean to invoke a *Star Wars* level of good versus evil. If you don't like the word "good," you can go with "whole," "complete," and "okay as is."

Let's put it together now. Instead of walking around feeling shitty about yourself because you aren't the most productive person, or you don't have the clearest skin, or you have significantly fewer Instagram followers than your peers, you are in fact fundamentally, primordially, and innately whole, good, and complete as is.

This basic goodness is your birthright. And while I come from a Buddhist background (born and raised, more on that later), this isn't even a Buddhist belief. It's an experience that anyone can have. In fact, you yourself can have it when you get out of your own way long enough to simply rest in the present moment.

And this, my friend, is why we meditate. We meditate to reveal that most basic part of ourselves: the part that is inherently okay, that allows us to experience ourselves and our world as good as is.

Okay, sure—there is a lot of science about meditation that says if you do a little bit of it every day, you see increased gray matter in the hippocampus of the brain and more activity in the anterior cingulate cortex. So much of the research that has come out falls under the general heading of "stress reduction," which is what makes meditation so sexy these days. For non-neuroscientists like me, that means you end up sleeping better, strengthening your immune system, and in general being less anxious. That's great. But in my experience, that's actually pretty surface level.

If you are the sort of person who struggles with self-doubt and self-worth, who is pretty damn mean to yourself in the comfort of your own head, or who is indeed stressed-out all the time, boy do I have good news for you: *that's not actually who you are.*

You are not incompetent.

You are not lazy.

You are not an anxious person.

These are simply stories that you tell yourself. The beauty of this realization is that you can choose to stop reinforcing these stories.

This book is here to guide you in redirecting your mental energy. It offers practical tools to help you spend more of your waking hours connecting with your inherent goodness and less time creating suffering in your own mind.

I've been grappling with this concept of basic goodness since childhood, and now that I'm in my forties I feel confident in its truth. I've seen people's lives transform when they embrace this idea.

Watching my two-year-old daughter has only reinforced my belief in basic goodness. She hasn't been told she's inadequate or lazy, and she hasn't learned to doubt herself. She simply radiates joy and confidence, fully at ease in her own skin.

We were all born with this same understanding of basic goodness, but over time we've learned behaviors that distance us from it. Now, it's time to unlearn these behaviors and return to who we truly are. It's time to rub away the clay and reveal the gold underneath.

Thank you for joining me on this journey. By the end of this book, I am confident you'll understand basic goodness not as an abstract idea but as a lived experience, something you feel in your heart because you've touched it directly.

I may not know you personally (yet; I hope to someday), but I do know this: you are basically good. So am I. Let's begin there.

2 THE ENTIRE BUDDHIST PATH IN TWO PAGES

I've been studying Buddhism for over thirty years now, and here's my complete summary of everything I've seen and heard and experienced:

Step 1: You Discover Basic Goodness

This is where the journey begins—with a direct experience of your own basic goodness. Meditation provides the framework for this discovery, as it allows you to sit with yourself, undistracted. In these moments, you can start to notice the natural goodness beneath all your doubts, worries, and mental habits. It's less about finding something new and more about peeling back the layers to reveal what's already there. When you feel even a glimpse of this innate goodness, you start to see how it can be a source of peace and stability. This is where things get juicy.

Step 2: You Deepen Your Relationship with Basic Goodness

Once you've experienced a sense of basic goodness, the Buddhist path provides a variety of tools to deepen your understanding. Books, retreats, and teachings all offer insights and practices, and they are all meant to help you reconnect with your innate nature more fully and frequently. These are not just intellectual exercises; they're skillful means—ways of training your mind and heart to recognize goodness within you, even in difficult moments. Over time, you'll find yourself returning to that sense of basic goodness with increasing ease.

Step 3: You Live Your Life Through the Lens of Basic Goodness

As your relationship with basic goodness grows, it begins to transform how you approach life. You start to notice your interactions, decisions, and even your self-talk shifting. When you trust in your own goodness, you stop constantly seeking validation from the outside world or feeling the need to prove your worth. Instead, you bring compassion and kindness to your relationships at work, in your family, and with friends. You see others—everyone really—as fundamentally good as well, even if they've covered that up with their own layers of hurt or insecurity. Living this way opens up a sense of spaciousness, a life less dominated by anxiety and more focused on connection, presence, and peace.

Let's unpack each of these steps a little more.

3 YOU DISCOVER BASIC GOODNESS

Years ago, I was leading a weekend meditation retreat. After a full Saturday of sitting, a woman raised her hand and asked, "So . . . is this it?"

I asked her what she meant.

"Sitting all day, resting with the breath, getting distracted, coming back to the breath. Is this it?"

I laughed, which made her laugh too. "Yes," I said, "this is basically it."

I used that word—*basically*—intentionally and explained how meditation is a tool to help us discover basic goodness for ourselves. Instead of being just a theory, meditation is a way to unlock a deeper understanding of who we truly are through our own experience.

"Were there moments today when you were able to relax and just be present?" I asked.

She nodded enthusiastically, and I asked her what those moments felt like.

"I felt okay," she replied.

"That's it," I confirmed. "That's the whole point. In these moments of being fully present, we discover that when we get out of our own way, we're okay. We're good as is. It's simple and yet it's magic at the same time."

For me, writing books on meditation is both fun and frustrating. The frustrating part is that I can write all the flowery prose in the world to try to convince people to meditate, but if they don't sit down and actually practice, everything else in the book becomes an intellectual exercise and isn't as helpful as I would hope.

The fun part is that sometimes people actually take my advice and meditate. When they do, they realize that basic goodness isn't just a philosophical idea—it's an experience they have. They write to tell me that this "whole meditation thing" has truly changed their lives for the better, and it's incredibly rewarding to hear that.

So much of the scientific research around mindfulness meditation tells us that there are objectively real changes that occur in our brain . . . after eight or so weeks. For example, we create new neural pathways that help us let go of stressful thoughts more easily and experience greater relaxation.

I come bearing good news for the impatient among us: you don't have to wait eight weeks to experience basic goodness. You can do that today, no neural rewiring required because, remember, this is already foundational to who you are.

You can sit down and do mindfulness meditation, and, in the moments in between focusing on work and dating, you might just rest with the breath for a moment. When you're there, fully in the present moment, you very well might have the same thought as that woman did: "Huh. Right now? I am okay."

With that in mind, here's a simple mindfulness meditation practice to try today.

Mindfulness Meditation Practice

1. Take a Relaxed and Uplifted Posture

If you are in a chair, you can place your feet firmly on the ground, about hips-width apart. If you sit on a cushion, make sure it's firm enough that you don't sink all the way to the floor. You want to be able to sit with your legs loosely crossed with your knees dropping a little below your hips.

From that strong base, elongate upward through the spine. You can imagine a string at the top of your head, pulling you straight up, allowing for the spine's natural curvature.

Relax the muscles in your shoulders, back, and arms. You can even drop your hands at your sides for a second, lifting the hands up at the axis point of the elbows and dropping them palms down on your thighs. This is a natural resting spot that will allow for additional support for the back (some of us aren't used to sitting up straight, despite any admonishments from our parents growing up).

Let your head rest atop your spine, with your chin slightly tucked. Soften the muscles in your face—unfurrow your forehead; relax around your eyes, cheeks, and jaw. It's okay if your jaw hangs open slightly; that's part of relaxing.

One potentially surprising note on your eyes: if you usually meditate with your eyes closed, I won't stop you. But generally, we keep our eyes open in meditation. This isn't about shutting out the world—it's about learning to be present with all of it.

Sound might be distracting, but we don't plug our ears to meditate, right? It's the same with sight. If open eyes make you feel a little more distracted, that's fine! We're not trying to be undisturbed meditators; we're trying to be ourselves, fully. Rest your gaze a few feet ahead, in a relaxed, soft focus.

2. Connect with the Natural Sensation of Your Breath

The entire time you've been reading this book, you have also been breathing. This is why the breath is a perfect object for our meditation. We don't need to do or generate anything; it is already happening.

All we have to do is drop into experiencing the breath. The other day, my friend and fellow Buddhist author Susan Piver visited The Basic Goodness Collective, the online community where I serve as the head teacher. She led the group in a meditation and wisely said to this group of experienced meditators, "To begin, stop trying to meditate."

It's genius advice because the main obstacle to relaxing with the breath is our urge to *do something* with it. But mindfulness meditation isn't about doing—it's about resting.

So I'll say it again: We are not here to achieve, produce, or even *do* anything in meditation. We are learning to relax long enough to bear witness to the present moment in its infinite joy and beauty. So don't try to do something with the breath. Don't control the breath. Don't even aim to think about the breath. Just be present to however the breath is flowing for you.

My teacher, Dza Kilung Rinpoche, once put it this way: "Sometimes it may seem that meditation means trying to do something different—to be something different. But it's not that way. What we're really trying to do is to be what we already are. We discover the true nature of mind instead of trying to be something else."

If you are the sort of person who does have a tendency to overthink things (I'm with you, don't worry), here's a little exercise to help you settle into the breath:

- First, bring your full attention to the top of your head for about ten seconds.
- Next, focus on your right knee for the same amount of time.

- Then shift your attention to your left thumb.
- Finally, bring your attention to your breath.

However you experience your breath—whether it's the coolness as it leaves your nose, the soft exhale from your mouth, or the rise and fall of your belly—is just right. Rest your attention there, simply being present with it.

3. When You Get Pulled Away from the Present Moment, Come Back

A common complaint about meditation is that we think it should always feel peaceful and as relaxing as a massage, but when we sit down we're shocked by how many thoughts we have. Here's a huge meditation secret: Thoughts are not a problem. They are not something to be overcome. In fact, you will always have thoughts (I'm sorry).

The act of meditation is to be present to an object of our attention—here, the breath—and when we get distracted, we come home to it once more. In other words, the getting distracted and coming back is a major part of the overall experience.

You will have thoughts. Some will be alluring, such as replaying a fun party you went to or fantasizing about a vacation. Others will be stressful, where you catch yourself spinning out about a work meeting or strategizing every potential way your dinner with family can go. *This is normal.*

I can't emphasize enough how normal it is to have a bazillion thoughts when you sit down to meditate. It's not that meditation has made you have more thoughts; it's that they are always there and you are just slowing down long enough to realize they exist. It's like a fish floating down the stream of a river; only when they pause do they actually feel the pull of the current itself.

At first, you may think there's something wrong with you that you can't simply be with the breath. Yet how much time have you spent doing that in the past? Likely not much.

Years ago, I took up CrossFit (and it only took me three chapters to mention it). I was training with a man named Nolan who, after I was done deadlifting a heavy weight, asked me how it felt. I was honest: "Deeply uncomfortable."

"Well," Nolan skillfully said, "how many times have you done that movement before?"

"Including the three reps we just did?" I replied. "Three."

He was quick to point out that doing anything new a few times will naturally be uncomfortable. I persisted and now, a few years later, my body naturally bends and shapes itself to deadlift like I was somehow born to do it. If you've ever seen a photo of me, you know I was indeed not born to do it, so this is impressive to me.

I mention this story because getting going with meditation is very similar. At first it feels awkward and our myriad expectations about what it *should* look and feel like get in the way of what it's actually like: a deeply uncomfortable getting-to-know-you process where we meet our own mind and heart in a visceral way.

If you have a lot of thoughts in meditation, there is nothing wrong with you. The way we relate to them is with incredible gentleness and discipline. When you notice that you have drifted off, just silently say to yourself, "Thinking." Then come back to the breath.

This act of acknowledging the thought and coming back to the breath will happen a lot at first, so don't freak out. If you're looking for a hack to make it easier, that's the gentleness thing I just mentioned. Say "thinking" very gently and remember that having thoughts is not a problem. It's a natural expression of the energy of your mind.

The discipline aspect is that we don't want to let the mind wander too far off. Some thoughts, as I noted, are pretty alluring. That sexual fantasy? It's fun. You don't necessarily want to come back to the boring old breath. But if we want to learn to rest with who we truly are, then we need to apply some discipline by acknowledging we drifted off—"thinking"—and then starting fresh with the breath.

To begin, I recommend doing ten minutes a day of meditation. I say this because we all have ten minutes. Even the busiest among us can find ten minutes by waking up a little early or watching one less episode of our show at night. Parents sometimes fight me on this, but now that I've joined your ranks I can affirm: we all can find ten minutes. Set a timer and allow yourself to simply be present with your breath and this moment, meeting it where it is.

Sometimes people want to start with guided meditation because ten minutes alone with themselves doing a new thing is understandably a bit intimidating. I have recorded a simple guided breathing meditation that is spacious and covers this particular technique, which you can access at lodrorinzler.com/youaregood.

When we meditate, we have moments when we're just, well, here. We're present with things as they are. We're not so lost in our head, and as a result we feel a certain level of contentment and energy that can be described as—you guessed it—basic goodness.

Sitting regularly, resting with the breath, getting distracted, and coming back to the breath. Remember how that woman asked me if this is it?

If you want to connect to basic goodness? Yes, this is it.

4 YOU DEEPEN YOUR RELATIONSHIP WITH BASIC GOODNESS

It's said that the Buddha offered 84,000 skillful ways for us to wake up to our true nature, to our basic goodness. It's not that we need to practice all 84,000 methods to achieve this but that there are simply that many pathways for us to arrive there.

To give a silly example, it's a bit like saying there are 84,000 ways to peel a banana. You could use your hands or a knife or, I suppose, a vegetable peeler. The tool itself isn't what matters—it's that, however you go about it, you get through the skin to the goodness underneath. Once you realize there's something worthwhile beneath the surface, you say, "Whoa, this is what the whole thing is about!" Then, naturally, you're motivated to keep peeling.

The same can be said for the entirety of the Buddhist path. For us, once we have had an initial discovery of our own basic goodness, everything from that moment on is about us deepening our relationship with and stabilizing this sense of who we truly are. Like the banana skin, this journey is less about adding layers and more about peeling them away to reveal what's already there.

Rather than exploring all 84,000 methods, let's break down the ways to deepen our connection with basic goodness into two broad categories: meditation and postmeditation.

Meditation is a powerful way to awaken to our natural state, that of inherent goodness. Mindfulness meditation, in particular, can offer a simple and direct path to living in alignment with this basic nature. That means we could spend decades practicing mindfulness meditation and, as long as we are engaging in that tool as a means to wake up to who we truly are, we will live a life based in basic goodness.

Just today, a meditation student of mine shared something very real: mindfulness meditation can be, well, boring at times. Thankfully, he was cool with that, but I know many people, after trying mindfulness a few times, end up wanting something more exciting. They might crave a mantra or a guided visualization tailored to their personal struggles.

Listen, we could engage in other types of meditation, such as loving-kindness (we'll get into this in chapter 9) or visualizations, and they can be helpful. But here's the thing: when we finish repeating the mantra or dissolve the visualization, what remains? Our own basic goodness. That's the heart of it.

That's why, instead of seeking out the coolest, sexiest meditation, or flitting from one technique to the next in the hope that something will feel easy to you, I always recommend the (sometimes) boring, (sometimes) hard work of mindfulness meditation. It wakes you up to who you genuinely are in an extremely straightforward manner. That's meditation.

Postmeditation refers to the rest of our waking hours—the time when we're out in the world. These, too, are opportunities to strengthen our connection to basic goodness. At the end of this section, I'll list a few specific postmeditation practices, but for now, here's a preview. It might mean spending quality time with loved ones and truly soaking in their company. It could look like taking a walk in nature and letting go of your usual preoccupations. Even now, simply taking a moment to stretch and tune in to your body without worrying about what comes next can open up a sense of connection to basic goodness.

In these sorts of scenarios we are not doing something very different than what we do in meditation. We acknowledge that we get pulled off into thinking about the past or the future and then come back to what is occurring in the present moment. We stay here long enough to enjoy it and experience who we truly are. The practice is that instead of shedding banana skin, we are shedding anything that separates us from resting in the present.

All of this is to say that building a relationship with basic goodness isn't so different from developing any other meaningful connection. Imagine meeting a new friend you genuinely like. You wouldn't walk away from them and say, "That's nice, but I should probably spend more time stressing about work." You would make a point to reconnect with them more frequently. The more time you spend with that friend the better you get to know them and the more you feel supported by them. In fact, as the relationship deepens, you find yourself wanting to be around them more.

The same goes for our relationship with basic goodness. Once we've caught a glimpse of it, it's up to us to decide how much time and energy we want to invest in coming back to that experience. We could choose to spend our mental energy pursuing more possessions, achievements, or distractions. Many people do just that, keeping themselves busy with the endless to-do lists and worries of modern life. Alternatively, we can make a wiser choice and say, "I'd like to get to know you better, basic goodness."

The amazing thing here is that when we look at everything the Buddha taught and all the ways we could cultivate a relationship with our awakened state, we find that our entire life—in meditation and in postmeditation—is filled with opportunities to release our worries and rest in this innate goodness.

In every moment, whether in meditation or during the most hectic parts of our day, we have a choice. We can allow ourselves to get lost in thoughts about the past or the future, following narratives in our mind that aren't unfolding in the present. Or we can wake up to the here and now, where we find that we're okay as we are. We can pause and rest in basic goodness, learning to trust and savor it, letting it become the foundational relationship we return to again and again.

5 YOU LIVE YOUR LIFE THROUGH THE LENS OF BASIC GOODNESS

By way of review, we have covered the first two steps of the entire spiritual path:

Step 1: You discover basic goodness.
Step 2: You deepen your relationship with basic goodness.

Once we start exploring basic goodness in our meditation and our daily interactions, we come to the fruition of our meditative journey: you live your life through the lens of basic goodness.

I have this pair of glasses that, when I go into the sunlight, automatically become sunglasses. The lens darkens and everything I see is subtly changed as a result.

Most of us move through the world with an invisible set of lenses too, but instead of filtering out glare, they filter reality through stress and anxiety. For instance, let's say you open your email and see a message from your boss. Right away, your mind races: *Is this good or bad? Am I in trouble?* The worry takes root, coloring your experience until you finally read the email, maybe only to discover it's harmless.

Even if you're having lunch with friends, the mind keeps circling back to the worry, pulling you out of the present and tinting everything with unease. You are no longer seeing your world through the lens of clarity; you're seeing it through your anxiety, and it's f-ing miserable.

Unfortunately, most of us do this constantly. The Buddha taught that as we navigate the world we bounce between three reactions:

- I like this (this is pleasant).
- I don't like this (this is unpleasant).
- I'll ignore this (this is neutral).

A small example. Recently, while teaching a meditation class at home, I heard my wife's car pulling into the driveway. My initial reaction was positive. I like my wife and was glad she was home. But then I remembered my large puppy, June, was sitting beside me. The moment June realized my wife was home, she started whining and barking, interrupting the session. My reaction shifted to dislike. Meanwhile, a few other cars passed the house and I actively ignored them, staying focused on my teaching. Within that thirty-second window, I moved through all three reactions: like, dislike, and ignore.

While this example may seem minor—no one was really bothered by June's excitement—it illustrates the fundamental ways we interact with the world. These responses—pleasant, unpleasant, and neutral—are the seeds of what the Buddha called the "three root poisons." These can grow into more entrenched patterns and, depending on the translation, are known as:

- passion or attachment
- anger or aggression
- ignorance or prejudice

Passion is a fancy way of saying "I want things to go my way." It's natural to think of passion as something positive—after all, don't we want passion in our relationships or our creative pursuits? But this particular form of passion locks us into rigid expectations, creating suffering when reality doesn't align with our wishes.

For example, you like the person you went on a date with. Cool! That's not this root poison. That's a free-flowing emotional state. It's when "I like them" becomes "They *have* to be my next big relationship" that you start to turn an interest into a new form of suffering. A pleasant experience has become a fixation. Specifically, you may fixate on how often they text you and what they say, and all of a sudden passion has solidified and given birth to anxiety and worry.

And when that person hasn't texted back in days? When you are ready to dismiss them outright for being a jerk who ghosts people? That's anger and aggression arising. Then, just as the story solidifies in your mind, they text back with a simple "I'm so sorry! I've been sick in bed all week." And—pop!—the bubble of anger bursts. Here, we've moved from passion to aggression, only to find that our attachment and irritation were based on incomplete information, leading us into the third poison: ignorance.

While you were caught up in this emotional spiral, life continued around you. But in this distracted state, many of us zone out, missing what's happening in real time. These root poisons—passion, anger, and ignorance—cloud our mental lenses, keeping us hooked on worries, desires, and assumptions. It's a cycle that leaves us exhausted and disconnected. We end up operating like zombies, marching through the day without any sense of connection to what's happening around us.

Here's the encouraging part: meditation offers us a way to step out of these clouded perceptions and see things as they truly are. Meditation teaches us to catch ourselves each time we get lost in thought and gently come back to the present. Each time we do this, we're literally rewiring our brains, training ourselves to live in the here and now instead of being pulled around by our reactive thoughts. Gradually, as we practice returning to the present in meditation, we find ourselves doing the same off the cushion, becoming more naturally grounded and clear-minded in our everyday lives.

When we go out for dinner with friends, for example, we're genuinely there with them, listening, laughing, and enjoying their company. We savor the taste of our food. We leave feeling uplifted, not drained. This simple act of showing up fully, without the tinted lens of stress or worry, is the path to living a life aligned with our basic goodness.

The more we remain open to the present moment, on and off the meditation cushion, the more we relax into our experience of basic goodness. We feel whole, complete, and healthy in our skin. Simple activities, such as walking the dog or sipping morning coffee, begin to feel extraordinary. They are very ordinary activities, but the extra here is that we are fully present for them and, as a result, they become a reflection of our experience of basic goodness.

As we deepen our relationship with basic goodness over the course of our lives, we see it affects not only these ordinary aspects of our day but all of our relationships. We begin to recognize the basic goodness of everyone around us and the basic goodness of society overall. Instead of viewing the world through the lens of passion, aggression, or ignorance, we see everything we encounter as a reflection of the basic goodness of all sentient beings.

6 BASIC GOODNESS ISN'T BUDDHIST

The funny thing about the term "basic goodness" is that it doesn't seem extremely Buddhist. And it's not! The Buddha didn't invent basic goodness any more than Isaac Newton invented gravity. It wasn't a philosophical point he came up with or a dogmatic principle he made people believe. Quite the opposite. It was something he experienced and then was able to point out the truth of to other people.

After he attained enlightenment, 2,600 years ago, the Buddha emerged from a long meditation session and went in search of a group of ascetics with whom he used to practice. These gentlemen had previously written the Buddha off. They were diehard "torture yourself in the name of spirituality" types, and he had taken some food as sustenance, which in this rigorously ascetic community was considered a huge no-no. As a result, they thought of him as a fraud.

Yet as he approached them, they saw that something had changed within him. They could tell he had gone through a major spiritual experience, and they were magnetized to him. As a result, they threw away their preconceived notions about him and approached, asking him to teach them so that they might follow in his footsteps.

At that moment, the Buddha could have done any number of things. He could have proclaimed that they bow before him and worship him as a god. He could have given them a list of dos and don'ts. He could have specified something they had to do every Sunday. Instead, he said, "Let me tell you, let me teach you. And if you listen and learn and practice as I tell you, very soon you will know for yourselves, not in some future life but here and now in this present lifetime, that what I say is true."[1] In other words, he asked them to test the mettle of his teachings and make sure that whatever he said was true to their own lived experience.

I can't overemphasize the importance of this distinction. It is the difference between, for example, the notion that you read a book like this one to gain knowledge versus reading it to help you realize something that is true about yourself and the world around you. It's the difference between intellectual understanding and experiential understanding.

Having issued the invitation to study with him, the Buddha then proceeded to teach the Four Noble Truths:

1. There is suffering. It exists. Pain and discomfort are unavoidable parts of life (I'm sorry).
2. This suffering arises as a result of ignorance about how things truly are. We always crave for things to be a little different and actively ignore the reality of our situation.
3. The good news? We don't have to perpetuate this suffering. We can awaken to our nature—our basic goodness—and to reality itself.
4. There is a path that we can follow to do exactly that, which is everything the Buddha taught thereafter.

The Buddha didn't negate that pain and discomfort are a part of everyday life. He knew it. You know it. I know it. That's the unfortunate reality of things. But that's not the end of the story. We suffer because we always crave for things to be like we want them to be instead of aiming to meet them as they are.

The third noble truth is that we are not our suffering. That's not actually who and what we are! We are, in fact, basically good. We are basically wakeful. In other words, we are already enlightened. We just need to discover it.

Which brings us to the fourth truth, which is everything he taught from that day forth that is meant to help us reconnect to our true nature, our own goodness.

To circle back to my initial point, the Buddha didn't invent basic goodness; he discovered it for himself. Once he discovered it, he realized this is a human experience that any one of us can tap into.

All the Buddha did is offer teachings so that we could discover basic goodness too. In this way, Buddhism is not some religion that you have to follow on blind faith, without examination. It's a path of practices and teachings that detail different ways to help you wake up your mind and heart and reconnect to your inherent nature.

Here's a fun additional part of the story. The Buddha wasn't some god. He wasn't an alien who came down to save us. He was a human being, just like you and me. *He was just like you and me.* He grew up with a difficult family situation. He fled that to try something else. He dabbled in all manner of spirituality before settling into this meditation thing. He was an incredibly *human* human.

What he discovered in his path of meditation is what we can discover in our path of meditation today: underneath the swirling layers of passion, aggression, and ignorance there is an unshakable wakefulness. Buddha was not his name. Translated from the Sanskrit, that honorific title simply means "awake." A man named Siddhartha Gautama became awake to his own nature and the nature of everything around him and lived a life based in that experience. That is what enlightenment is and that is why we call him "the awakened one" or "the Buddha."

The only difference between him and you and me? We are not *currently* living in complete alignment with our innate nature, our inherent buddhahood, also known as our buddha nature.

If the man who became the Buddha did the exact same practice we are doing, and was just as human as we are, then with my brilliant powers of deduction I can confidently say that we possess the same nature and ability to wake up to that nature as the Buddha did.

He possessed buddha nature, sometimes referred to as basic goodness. So do we. We follow in his footsteps by doing these practices and studying his words, and we can wake up in just as big a way. Just like Siddhartha, we are both very human humans now as well as future buddhas in the making.

7 HOW SOCIETY MESSES US UP

"Lodro," you might say, "okay, sure, there was a guy 2,600 years ago who woke up to basic goodness, and maybe I've felt some moments of peace in meditation that hinted at it. But is that really who I am? Do I really have this basic goodness at my core?"

Fair question. It's one thing to read about basic goodness or experience glimpses of it, and another thing entirely to trust it as your true nature. That trust, in fact, is exactly what society undermines from an early age.

When I take my daughter to the playground, I believe that she doesn't toddle around the playground thinking, "Wow. That kid really has much nicer clothes than I do. I bet she has more toys than I do and that I will never have enough clothes and toys." No. My guess is that she is simply present and delighted to be at the playground. I am also going to guess that this experience was true for you too when you were very young. In those early years, we're naturally attuned to the present moment and able to delight in it. We stay in contact with our own sense of basic goodness—our inherent sense that we're okay just as we are.

But then, somewhere along the way, society steps in and interrupts that connection. Maybe it's something your parents said, an incident at school, or the teachings of a religious institution. Whatever the source, at some point most of us internalize the message "I am not enough as I am." To be clear, this is not innate; it is learned behavior. You took on ideas and opinions about how you don't have everything you need internally and ought to look outside of yourself for validation and happiness.

Recently my friend Neil came for a visit. He once told me that as a gay man, he grew up afraid of what people would think about him if they knew who he really was. Just by virtue of being attracted to men, societal messaging taught him that something was broken inside him. Ultimately, Neil overcame that messaging and came out.

However, years later when he first heard the teachings on basic goodness, he was stunned. "I don't think I ever heard anything like it," he said. "Is this how people have been moving through the world, with a sense that they are like fundamentally worthy and not just inherently deserving of shame and blame?" Neil realized that he had been okay all along. That the problem wasn't him. He didn't need to be fixed. That he has always, by virtue of being who he is, been whole and complete as is.

Even if you did not receive messaging exactly like Neil's, that some part of who you are is wrong or in need of fixing, I imagine that story resonates. We have all, at some point in our lives, felt like something was out of alignment between us and the world around us and that *we* were the problem, not the society encouraging us to conform or change who we are.

The bummer is that our whole capitalistic system is built around this basic confusion around our sense of enoughness. We are told the lie that we don't have enough and need something external to us to make us whole, be it by the cosmetics industry or the diet industry or, to be a little shady for a moment, some areas of the wellness industry. Companies make money off the idea that you're basically messed up and, lo and behold, if you come to them, they have something that can fix you.

Take the fitness industry, for example. If we all felt our bodies were perfect just as they are, companies selling weight-loss medicines and certain types of programs would sink into the ocean. This isn't a knock against fitness as a whole; many fitness companies celebrate self-acceptance and health. But there's a segment of it, as in any industry, that depends on us believing we're not enough. And that story seeps into every part of our lives:

- In education, we're told, "If you don't excel academically, you'll never amount to anything."
- In work, we hear, "You need a high-paying job to be truly comfortable. And if you get that, level up and aspire to a better, higher-paying one."
- In romance, we fear, "If you don't find a partner by a certain age, you're going to end up lonely and unfulfilled. You'll die alone."

If we gave up the ghost on even one of these stories—if we stopped believing in one source of our "not enoughness"—we might start to see that these insecurities don't come from our true nature but from society's voice whispering in our ears for far too long. The refrain is always, you'll be happy when . . .

- . . . you find a partner.
- . . . you get a promotion.
- . . . you finally fit into that size, drive that car, or live in that neighborhood.

From a young age, we're bombarded by media, ads, social conditioning, and even well-meaning parental advice that builds up this idea that we're incomplete as we are. Then we all have that moment when we realize someone else has nicer clothes or better toys, or we start comparing our appearance, academic success, or athletic prowess to that of others. That's often when we begin to doubt our basic goodness, and this leads to a lack of confidence and a feeling of deficiency.

Whether there was one incident or many that interrupted the connection to basic goodness, once we begin to doubt it, we tend to spiral forward in that direction. You likely spent decades soaking in the point of view of "I'm not good enough. I am not enough. I don't have enough and I likely never will."

On top of that, society keeps up a confusing double message: while we're told we're not enough and need to look outside ourselves for happiness, we're also told that if we work hard, dream big, and believe in ourselves, we can achieve anything. This sets us up for constant striving. It's impossible to scroll through social media without seeing a cheerful post that says something like, "Believe it and you'll achieve it!" But as much as I've believed in my own potential to grow six feet tall, I somehow remain five-foot-seven.

We are in a system in which we spend all of our waking hours striving to do more, achieve more, and produce more in the hope that the next big thing outside of us—that relationship, degree, or house—will finally make us feel whole and happy.

Well, let me ask you: How is that working out for you?

If you've reached a milestone you once dreamed of, you may have found that it only satisfied you temporarily. You got that relationship, but it wasn't perfect. You got the degree, but it left you with debt. The new house is nice, but now you're comparing it to your neighbor's. You realize that as long as you're looking for validation and happiness from outside, there will always be another goal to chase, another "if only."

I am so sorry. I really am. It's messed up that you have been told that you're not enough and that you need to go outside of yourself for any chance of feeling whole. It's simply not true, but it's told to us all the time.

The thing that the Buddha discovered, that thing you can or perhaps already have discovered in meditation yourself—basic goodness—flies in the face of the way you were raised. Just because you were forced out of your connection with basic goodness once does not mean that you have to live the rest of your life that way.

Basic goodness is still there, beneath all the societal conditioning. You, right now, can choose to lean into that experience and let go of the stories that no longer serve you. When you choose to loosen the hold of those stories, you slice through the delusion of not enough, showing you the contentment that's already possible—right here, right now.

8 THE TRAP OF DOUBT

There's a story I skipped over earlier, which adds a powerful dimension to understanding the Buddha's path to awakening. I picked up the story when he was already enlightened; this is a VH1 *Before They Were Stars* tale. Siddhartha Gautama—on the brink of enlightenment—was meditating under a tree, diving deeper into the realization of his true nature, his basic goodness. But then along came Mara.

In Buddhism, Mara is often called the king of the demons. He is the tempter. Does he actually exist in a physical form? Maybe! It doesn't actually matter for the sake of this story. But as the very embodiment of temptation, the way the tale goes is that he came across the person who was about to become a buddha and said, "No thank you. We won't be having any of that enlightenment business today."

Mara sent a range of alluring distractions Siddhartha's way, hoping to break his concentration. But Siddhartha remained steady. Next, Mara tried a different tactic, sending threats and frightening images, hoping fear might throw him off. Yet Siddhartha stayed grounded and present. In some versions of the story, these temptations take the form of beautiful women and terrifying demons. Whether literal or symbolic, the core message is that Siddhartha, on the verge of enlightenment, had to face these extreme tests.

This isn't so different from our own experiences in meditation. Just like Siddhartha, we might find ourselves lured away by pleasurable fantasies, drifting off into tempting daydreams. Or we might be jarred by painful memories or worries that feel unbearable. These deeply compelling thoughts are the same types of distractions Siddhartha faced in his last hours before enlightenment.

The final challenge from Mara was incredibly pointed and personal. It was an attack on Siddhartha's worthiness. To paraphrase Mara's taunt: "Who do you think you are, aiming to attain enlightenment? You? A prince? Mr. Privilege over here? After your whole fancy upbringing, you left that life behind and tried asceticism. You couldn't even stick to asceticism without breaking the rules by eating! Really, you think *you* are worthy of attaining enlightenment?"

At this point, Siddhartha did something remarkable. He touched the ground. In that simple, powerful gesture, it was as if he called the earth itself to bear witness to his inherent worthiness. By touching the ground, Siddhartha claimed his fundamental right to awaken—not because of what he'd done or achieved, but because of who he was. He recognized that as a human being, he was already innately good and worthy.

Once Siddhartha proclaimed his inherent worthiness, it's said that Mara freaked out and took off. He couldn't deal with this person who was so confident in his inherent self-worth.

This story speaks to a critical challenge in our own journey with basic goodness. Yes, we can get distracted by all the things we desire or want to get away from, sure. But the biggest obstacle to us realizing our true nature is often the trap of doubt.

The trap of doubt is different from the type of doubt we might normally encounter. For instance, if I put on a yellow sweater and look in the mirror, I might think, "I doubt this color suits me" (and I'd probably be right). That's a normal, insignificant kind of doubt. The trap of doubt is something far more toxic. It's that cruel inner voice that goes beyond a critique of an incidental item and insinuates something about your essential identity: "You're ugly and no one will ever find you attractive." This kind of doubt is deeper and much more damaging.

The trap of doubt is the whisper in your ear that says you are not enough, you don't have enough, and you will *never* be or have enough. It's the voice that criticizes you for every small misstep. It's the thoughts that pull you into comparing yourself to others and makes you feel less than others. And, frankly, it's bullshit.

After failing to shake Siddhartha with other temptations, Mara turned to the trap of doubt, hoping to make Siddhartha question his self-worth. "Who are you to attain enlightenment?" was Mara's taunt. That voice may sound familiar to us—it's often the same voice in our own heads, casting doubt on even the smallest aspirations:

"Who are you to ask for a raise? You've only worked this job for two years."

"Someone like you? Ask that person out? They'll definitely say no."

"You? You think you're the sort of person who can meditate? You are way too anxious and you'll never be able to experience a sense of peace."

There are countless versions of this self-defeating voice, and it all serves to pull us away from the present moment, drawing us into self-doubt and discouragement.

Because we have grown so accustomed to the trap of doubt, it will take some time to dismantle it. I think of it like a bear trap. Imagine you're walking through the woods, enjoying the peaceful surroundings, and then—snap—the trap of doubt springs shut. You begin to focus on how you messed up at work, and the trap has now clamped down on your leg. As you continue to perpetuate thoughts about what you got wrong, you thrash your leg around and the trap tightens and digs in deeper.

You can't escape the trap of doubt by thrashing against it, hoping it will magically release you. You need to reach down, find the release mechanism, and unlock it. Sounds simple, right? Yet if you had a bear trap on your leg and were reeling in pain, it would be hard to calm yourself and simply do it.

Similarly, when we are lost in the trap of doubt, thrashing around and beating ourselves up over something that may have happened years ago, all we have to do is cut through the story and come back to the present moment. It's simple, like pressing the release button on a physical trap, but we get so entangled in our pain that we often forget.

I know this one well. Few people are better at beating themselves up than I am. It's one of my superpowers. I'm half joking here, but when I do or say the wrong thing, particularly when it hurts someone, I spiral. And I've done that, to be clear. I am far from fully enlightened. This is what happens when we get confused about our basic nature. We make mistakes that can lead to pain for ourselves or others. In those moments, I tell myself I should be beyond this, that I shouldn't stumble like this, given my years of practice. But that's me, pulling the trap tighter and causing myself more pain.

When I'm caught in the trap of doubt, one prompt that helps me—maybe it will help you too—is to ask, "What is happening right now?" You might be driving, lost in a cycle of self-criticism, imagining all the ways people are judging you, and then, in that brief moment of awareness, you realize you're in the trap. At that point you can stop and ask, "What is happening right now?"

Right now you are driving. Your hands are on a steering wheel. Your body is breathing. Your foot is pressing on the gas or brake. A song is on the radio. This is what is actually happening right now. Coming back to the present moment in this way is like hitting the release on the trap of doubt. Those painful stories are what keep us bound, and when we drop them, the trap itself begins to dissolve.

As Mara set up the trap of doubt, taunting Siddhartha, the soon-to-be-buddha saw what was happening and didn't take the bait. That's what Siddhartha's famous touching-the-earth gesture was all about. It was him saying, "You think I'm not enough to attain enlightenment? Bullshit. I am inherently worthy and basically good." This simple act broke the hold of Mara's trap.

The trap of doubt is the primary obstacle to living your days in basic goodness. These self-aggressive thoughts are the main thing that prevents you from experiencing basic goodness. The good news here is that you created those thoughts. Those stories of not being enough are ones you internalized or came up with and are perpetuating today. You created the trap itself. That means you are the only one with the key and the power to release it and drag yourself out. So how do we start to dismantle the trap and release those Mara-like stories? Through meditation.

9 LEARNING TO LOVE ALL OF WHO YOU ARE

Years ago I coauthored *How to Love Yourself (and Sometimes Other People)* with my good friend Meggan Watterson. The second half of the title is tongue-in-cheek, but it touches on something crucial: if you can't extend love to yourself, you won't be able to offer it to others. It's like trying to pull water from a well that is completely empty.

When we were on tour for the book, we spoke at a Hay House conference with several other spiritual teachers. A friend made a great point during her talk: "You know how everyone always says you should love yourself more? Well, how come no one ever tells you *how* to actually do it?" Meggan and I exchanged a look. We felt we'd covered that in our book—it's right there in the title!

So here, right now, I'll tell you how to do it. Because the trap of doubt is strong, my friend, and we need multiple ways to unhook ourselves from it.

My favorite Tibetan word for meditation is *gom*. It can be translated as "become familiar with" or "familiarization." The more we become familiar with all of who we are in meditation, the more we befriend ourselves. The more we offer friendship to ourselves, the more we learn to love ourselves.

There likely isn't a single romantic partner or friend that you have met and immediately felt complete and total love for. Sure, there likely have been some people you connected to quite quickly and really hit it off with. But how did that initial connection blossom into love? Through spending time together.

When we meditate, we are spending time with ourselves and thus bearing witness to the good, bad, and ugly of it all. Like a lover or friend, we don't run away when we see things we feel an aversion to. We embrace that person, warts and all. Same thing here, only we are embracing all of who we ourselves are. Meditation, among other things, is a tried-and-true method for learning to love ourselves unconditionally.

The Buddha described four types of love, known as the four immeasurables, that are limitless in their scope:

- loving-kindness
- compassion
- sympathetic joy
- equanimity

We'll dive into compassion and sympathetic joy in a later chapter, when we explore different kinds of relationships, and we'll touch on equanimity when we discuss broader society. For now, let's focus on the practice of extending love to ourselves (and sometimes other people).

A moment ago I mentioned "the good, bad, and ugly of it all." From a Buddhist perspective, this can be reframed around the reactions we explored earlier: the parts of ourselves we like, the parts we don't like, and the parts we actively ignore. We all have them; it's normal! For example, a part of yourself that you like might be the one that excels at your job, or goes out of its way to help others, or is particularly talented at a given musical instrument or skill. A part that you may not like might be the one that is overly sarcastic or cutting, or says the wrong thing after a few drinks, or gossips way too much about other people.

Then there are the parts that we actively ignore, the ones that, say, instinctively reach for a phone whenever there's a lull, or that bite our nails when anxiety kicks in. These tendencies often go unnoticed until they're already in motion.

If we are going to aim to love ourselves, we can't just love the positive parts of who we are. We have to be there for and embrace the whole shebang. With that in mind, let's try a short meditation practice together.

Loving-Kindness for Yourself

"Loving-kindness" is a term you may have heard before. It's translated from the Pali word *metta,* which can also be translated as "kind friendliness." In essence we are saying that the root of love for ourselves and others is kind friendship.

The Buddha taught on loving-kindness in the *Karaniya Metta Sutta,* but it was only in the fifth century that Acariya Buddhaghosa formalized these teachings into the meditation on loving-kindness that we know and cherish today.

To start off, I recommend doing a few minutes of mindfulness meditation to truly land in your body. When you're ready, you can bring to mind a version of yourself that you really like. This could be the part of yourself that is a good friend, or is generous in a relationship, or something else entirely.

Holding this image in mind, you can make aspirations for the well-being of this specific part of you. The way to do this is to offer these phrases in your own mind or out loud at the volume just below a whisper:

May I feel happy

May I feel healthy

May I feel safe

May I feel peaceful

Repeat those phrases three times, pausing after each one for the aspiration to truly land in your being.

Take a deep breath, and on the out-breath just let that image you are holding go. Rest for a moment.

Now you can bring to mind a part of yourself that you don't normally look at. Maybe it's the part of you that habitually grabs your phone in uncomfortable moments, or it's the part that spends way too long doom-scrolling on social media, losing all track of time. Holding this part of yourself in mind, you can make the same aspiration:

May I feel happy

May I feel healthy

May I feel safe

May I feel peaceful

As before, repeat these phrases three times, acknowledging and wishing well this part of yourself.

Take another deep breath, and on the exhale let this image go.

One last part here. Bring to mind an aspect of yourself that you don't really like. This could be the part that has a really bad habit you don't know how to shake or the part that spends more money than you might like on things you absolutely don't need. Instead of judging this part of yourself, let's send it some loving-kindness:

May I feel happy

May I feel healthy

May I feel safe

May I feel peaceful

One more deep breath here, letting that part of yourself go on the out-breath.

To conclude, place your hands on your heart and make one final aspiration, this time for the totality of who you are. This includes the parts of yourself that you like, the parts you don't know very well, and the parts you have a hard time with:

May all of who I am feel happy

May all of who I am feel healthy

May all of who I am feel safe

May all of who I am feel peaceful

When you're ready, you can open your eyes or raise your gaze, moving out of the formal meditation.

This technique is a variation on the traditional loving-kindness practice. You can download it as well as the traditional practice at lodrorinzler.com/youaregood.

The more we engage in mindfulness meditation and loving-kindness for ourselves, the more we realize we can embrace all of who we are without judgment. That judgment leads us directly into the trap of doubt. If we can uproot it at the source, then this trap has no power over us. Through these meditation practices we can get to know, befriend, and ultimately learn to love all of who we are.

10 WORKING WITH GUILT AND SHAME

I did my first monthlong meditation retreat when I was seventeen years old. It was intense. The thing they never tell you about meditation retreats is that while you have a lot of hours on the cushion, they also include hours of practicing presence in daily activities—walking, eating, cleaning, and so on. There aren't a lot of fun distractions when you're on one of these things. There is a lot of room for the mind to wander off into thoughts (and thus a lot of opportunity to bring the mind back to the present).

About three weeks into this extremely spacious meditation retreat, I began reflecting on the girlfriend I had broken up with six months before. I decided that I'd been insensitive in how I'd broken up with her and began to feel guilty. Once I had made up my mind that I had done a bad thing, I continued to dwell on that bad thing for several days, beating myself up about it like no one's business. I finally convinced myself that once I was out of that meditation retreat I would apologize to my ex in person for the way things ended. Having acknowledged my seeming misdeed and hatched a plan to aim for amends, I began to drop the stories I was telling myself and relax a little.

When I got home and school started again, I was ready to reach out—only to find that she'd moved away over the summer, as her father had gotten a new job elsewhere. This was before social media, so with no way to contact her, I went back to feeling bad about it . . . for a decade.

Flash forward to me hanging out in my college dorm room in my twenties when I got a notification on Facebook: a friend request from my ex. We began chatting on the site, becoming reacquainted. It wasn't long into our exchange when I said, "Listen. I feel really badly about how I ended things between us. I know it's been years, but I'd like to catch up and apologize for real."

"That's funny," she replied, "I don't remember it like that at all. But it would be fun to catch up anyway!"

It turns out the thing that I had held on to for years, beating myself up about and feeling relentless guilt and shame over, wasn't even real. It was a story I had made up that wasn't her lived experience.

Now I'd love to say, "That's the last time guilt and shame got ahold of me," but that's not true. I continued to date and make mistakes and hurt myself and others. This is a part of being human and, thankfully, of growing up. The mistakes I make in my forties are significantly different, subtler, and less damaging than the ones I made in my twenties. Along the way, I've also continued to work with my finely honed ability to hold every mistake, whether it be from last week or ten years ago, against myself. I know for a fact that no one can beat me up or make me feel shittier about myself than I can, and I am actively working on letting those stories go.

I'm guessing you might be able to relate to this. You might have said or done something that you later deemed "bad," and as a result immediately began to build a case for why you are a bad person. This is something we all do.

Guilt and shame are the henchmen of the trap of doubt. There's basic goodness, and then something happens—a mistake, a misstep—that makes us question or feel disconnected from it. That could be saying something unkind, or sleeping with the wrong person, or acting out of line at work. Whatever it is, we all of a sudden don't feel very good, do we?

At that point, we could address the situation and move toward healing. If there's one thing I've learned over time it's that acknowledging when we do wrong, spending time in that realm of discomfort, and having tough conversations can help us grow in a positive direction. The alternative is almost too horrible to bear: we spiral into shame and guilt, leading us to believe that we are not basically good but basically bad, and if anyone knew what we said or did, they would not want to be friends with us or employ us or date us, and so on.

The American Buddhist nun Pema Chödrön wrote eloquently on this topic when she detailed the difference between negative and positive shame: "Negative shame is accompanied by guilt and self-denigration. It is pointless and doesn't help us even slightly." [1] It is, in other words, a waste of time and mental energy.

> Positive shame, on the other hand, is recognizing when we've harmed ourselves or anyone else and feeling sorry for having done so. It allows us to grow wiser from our mistakes. Eventually it dawns on us that we can regret causing harm without becoming weighed down by negative shame. Just seeing the hurt and heartbreak clearly motivates us to move on. By acknowledging what we did, cleanly and compassionately, we go forward.[2]

When confronting shame and guilt, I've found it helpful to face these feelings directly. As a prompt in that direction, I want to offer you a useful phrase, one that has helped me: "I too am human." This phrase reminds me that I am a fallible, learning human being. The beauty of this acknowledgment is that we can learn from mistakes and grow, moving toward further wakefulness and doing less harm to ourselves and others over time. When you feel lost in shame and guilt, try offering yourself this simple phrase of loving-kindness: "I too am human."

About a decade ago, while serving on the board of an aid organization for unhoused youth, I led a meditation for a group of teenagers. Afterward, our conversation turned to mistakes and how to handle them. One participant shared a piece of wisdom his grandmother had given him that I've never forgotten: "One hundred different mistakes are progressive. One hundred of the same mistake is regressive." In other words, making a mistake and learning from it—letting it change us for the better—is progress on the path of becoming more fully human. That growth puts us directly in touch with our basic goodness. But if we repeat a mistake without learning, it's regressive and we'll keep getting stuck in the same pain.

Learning from a mistake is different from drowning in shame and guilt. Shame and guilt have no place in true healing, whether it's for you or for other people. The more we uproot the stories we tell ourselves about how shitty we are, the closer we get to understanding what is actually happening versus our projected fears and judgments. With that clarity, we can correct our course and engage in meaningful healing work. Taking those steps brings us back into direct contact with our basic goodness.

11 PRACTICES FOR CONNECTING WITH YOUR BASIC GOODNESS

To reiterate, the best practice for connecting to basic goodness is mindfulness meditation. Loving-kindness meditation can also help us look at and embrace all the parts of who we are. That said, I want to offer a number of simple practices that can connect you with your basic goodness in the waking hours of the day when you are not meditating, plus one more traditional practice that you may find helpful.

Enjoy Your Coffee

When you have your morning beverage, just taste it. Maybe, like me, you're a coffee drinker, but tea works too. Start by feeling the warmth of the mug in your hands. Smell the aroma. When you have thoroughly enjoyed that, take a sip. Actually taste it. Relax into the experience. See if basic goodness can be found in this simple, present moment.

Feel Basic Goodness in the Body

Choose a short walk that you do routinely, like the walk from your apartment to the subway or from your front door to the car. It can be any number of things, like the walk from your car to the grocery store, but pick one.

For that walk, just walk. Feel the weight of your body as it moves through space. Notice the uncertainty as one foot leaves the ground, then lands again. Sense how your body balances and adjusts as you move. Be fully present for each step. See if basic goodness can be found by tuning in to your body.

Be Present While Getting Dressed

While we're often daydreaming about other things while we dress, you could be present even then. Instead of spacing out, feel the texture and weight of the clothes in your hands. Appreciate the shirt or pants before you put them on. Notice how they make you feel as you put them on.

A trick I learned in my frequently hungover twenties was to dress myself up when I was feeling down. I would put on a button-down shirt, a nice tie, and a blazer, and immediately, through engaging in that act, feel a bit more at home in my skin. By appreciating the clothes and the effect they had in uplifting me, I reconnected to my basic goodness.

Feel the Beat

Put on a song you enjoy. For the duration of the song, when your mind wanders, just come back to listening to that song. Think of it like meditation: instead of returning to the breath, you return to the music. For me, I have a particular recording of Lou Reed's *Perfect Day* that I enjoy practicing with. Enjoy the song fully. As you rest in enjoying the song, see if basic goodness naturally arises.

Take a Shower

The next time you hop in the shower, be present for the full duration of your time there. When you get in, actually feel the warm water hitting your skin. Allow that sensation to be the object of your attention. Tune in to the smell of the soap and shampoo. Allow yourself to experience all of the physical sensations that you normally tune out because you are too lost in your head. This time can feel like a gift to yourself, and basic goodness can be found in such a mundane, grounding activity.

Contemplate Death

Whoa. We went from coffee and short walks to talking about something no one wants to talk about. Once a week or so, I recommend engaging in a short death contemplation. The purpose of such a practice is not to freak us out about this thing that, by the way, does happen to literally everyone, but to remind us that we don't know how long we have in this life and so we must take advantage of each day.

To begin, sit in mindfulness meditation for a few minutes. When you're settled, contemplate this traditional verse:

> The whole world and its inhabitants are impermanent. In particular, the life of beings is like a bubble. Death comes without warning; this body will be a corpse. At that time the dharma will be my only help. I must practice it with exertion.[1]

Here, *dharma* refers to the teachings that help us wake up to who we truly are, to our own basic goodness. This verse acknowledges that everyone—we and all the beings we love—are unfortunately impermanent. Our lives are not very long and are as fragile as a bubble blown by a young child. We do not know when we will die, only that it is inevitable. We must use this time we do have—all the days and years—to wake up to who we truly are and live a life that we feel is meaningful.

How do we do contemplation practice? We recite the verse—either in its entirety or line by line, pausing along the way—and then rest. We do not intellectualize or overthink these phrases. We merely sit and bear witness to them, allowing whatever wisdom we possess to arise and engage with the verse.

This is a precious human life. How do you want to live it? In connection with basic goodness or stressed out and held by fear? Feeling into a determination to connect to our true nature helps us prioritize it over the trivialities of our existence.

If you engage in these six activities over the course of a week, you'll likely find your connection to your own basic goodness growing. Many of these practices involve things you already do, you're just shifting the way you approach them. Instead of letting daily routines become times when you check out or leave the present moment, let them bring you into direct contact with who you truly are.

PART TWO

EVERYONE ELSE IS BASICALLY GOOD

12 REALIZING THE GOODNESS OF OTHERS

Now we reach the plot twist: It's not just you who is basically good. It's me, plus your noisy neighbor, plus your crush, plus that politician that you think is completely horrible. It's everyone around us. Every single person possesses basic goodness.

The Buddhist teacher Tara Brach expressed this idea beautifully in her book *Trusting the Gold*: "For decades a prayer has circulated in the background of my daily life: May I trust my own goodness. May I see the goodness in others."[1]

This aspiration—the ability to see goodness in others as well as in ourselves—is essential to our growth in basic goodness. It's one thing to acknowledge that we may be—underneath all of our habitual bullshit—basically good. It's another to look around us and see that goodness in everyone else. "May I trust my own goodness" is the first big step in our spiritual development. "May I see the goodness in others" is the next.

Let's look closer at that word "others," because it includes three distinct groups:

- a small group we can call the "people I like"
- a (we hope) smaller group we can call the "people I don't like"
- and a massive, overlooked group called "everyone else"

The people we like might include friends, family, co-workers, and others. The people we dislike may be those who've hurt us—old high-school bullies or difficult colleagues. Then that last group of everyone else consists of those we usually don't consider enough to like or dislike, simply because we're busy ignoring them.

Do those three groups look familiar? If so, it's likely because whenever we look at the people around us, we unconsciously put them into these groups based on the three root poisons we discussed earlier: passion/attachment, anger/aggression, and ignorance/prejudice.

For instance, you walk down the street and see someone attractive; they get lumped into the "people I like" group due to a spark of passion. Someone loud and abrasive is yelling on the corner; they get lumped into the "people I don't like" group due to a spark of aggression. All the other people around you? They get filed under "everyone else," the people we ignore—our (lack of) perception shaped by the root poison of ignorance.

In the chapters ahead we will explore ways to recognize the basic goodness in each of these groups. With practice we can learn to see the goodness not just in the people we like but even in those we don't, and ultimately in everyone, whether we ever meet them or not.

13 AWAKENING TO BODHICHITTA

Before we dive into these three groups—people I like, people I dislike, and everyone else—I want to talk about a natural evolution that happens when we've been meditating for a bit: the birth of *bodhichitta*.

Have you ever had a moment when you get up from meditation, perhaps having had a glimpse of a connection to your basic goodness, and something really adorable happens? Your puppies begin roughhousing in an affectionate way, your kid says something delightfully quirky and sweet, or a family member calls just to check in on you. In that moment, your heart feels wide open and tender. This is bodhichitta.

The term *bodhichitta* combines two Sanskrit words: *bodhi*, meaning "open" or "awake," and *chitta*, meaning "heart/mind." There's not a lot of distinction between the mind and heart in this context. Putting that together, bodhichitta is our own open or awakened heart. It's the heart that feels tenderness for all the lovely and heartbreaking things life presents.

It's also the heart that grows ten times bigger reading news about people who are suffering overseas. It's even the heart that is able to muster a bit of compassion for someone who has wronged you. In other words, it's the expansive, vast heart that can accommodate everything, including the people I like, the people I dislike, and everyone else.

Bodhichitta is inseparable from basic goodness. It is when we feel fully rooted in our most authentic sense of self that we are naturally open and aware of others. We listen to them more and care more deeply.

The example of a first date comes to mind. Maybe you have shown up for a date nervous, disconnected from your sense of enoughness and basic goodness, already doubting that this person will like you for who you are. Because of that disconnect, you act out of your anxiety, interrupting them frequently or drinking too much to cover over nervous energy. It becomes awkward and you walk away feeling disappointed in yourself and the date overall.

Now imagine the same scenario after regular meditation practice. You enter the date grounded in your basic goodness—not puffed up by arrogance, mind you, but confident in the fact that you are enough as you are. As a result, you are more present with this person. You listen deeply to what they say and respond from a place of wholeness and consideration. At the end, because you have been so present, you feel more connected to this person and walk away feeling a bit more uplifted, regardless of whether this person is a match for you or not.

Our own connection (or lack thereof) to our basic goodness plays out in every relationship in our life. We either approach our relationships from a feeling of lack and a poverty mentality or a feeling of completeness and comfort in our own skin.

When we are rooted in our basic goodness, we simply feel like we have more to offer (dating or otherwise). Our heart is more relaxed and open, and this openness is the essence of bodhichitta. It is a tender, vulnerable feeling of love. It's the simple truth that our open hearts can accommodate everyone, so long as we remain connected to our true nature. Because we are so open, we are also more open to seeing the suffering of others and our heart goes out to them.

Someone who actively cultivates this open-hearted quality and works to benefit others is called a *bodhisattva*. *Bodhi*, as before, means "open" or "awake." *Sattva* is sometimes translated as "being" or even "warrior." In other words, a bodhisattva is an open-hearted warrior. Here "warrior" does not denote someone who goes to war with others but someone who battles against their own neurosis and confusion so as to awaken to their true nature and help others awaken as well.

The Tibetan Buddhist teacher Chögyam Trungpa Rinpoche once wrote, "The goal of warriorship is to express basic goodness in its most complete, fresh, and brilliant form. This is possible when you realize that you do not *possess* basic goodness but that you *are* the basic goodness itself. Therefore, training yourself to be a warrior is learning to rest in basic goodness, to rest in a complete state of simplicity."[1]

As we move forward, looking at how we relate to the people we like, dislike, and actively ignore, we can consider this role of bodhisattva and aspire to be bodhisattvas ourselves, undercutting our confusion and anxiety so that we may rest in simplicity and more fully connect with and be of benefit to everyone we encounter.

Three Methods for Rousing Bodhichitta

There are a bazillion ways one could connect to an open and awake heart. However, there are three traditional methods that have been around for centuries that I want to share so that you have a specific practice for connecting to that limitless source of love more regularly.

1. Contemplating Kindness

The first is to contemplate the great kindness that has been shown to us by an individual. Traditionally, this would be a benefactor who provided monks with meals, allowing them time for practice. In today's world, you might bring to mind someone who has shown you ongoing support throughout your life. This could be a good friend who has seen you through many a heartbreak, or a romantic partner or a family member who has consistently looked out for you. Whoever comes to mind for you upon reading this paragraph is likely a good person to work with.

2. Gratitude for Our Teachers

The second form of rousing bodhichitta, from a traditional perspective, would be bringing to mind the teachers who have shown you great wisdom and kindness through offering the Dharma, or teachings of the Buddha. Here, you may prefer to bring to mind a person who has offered you valuable guidance, such as a teacher or mentor who's been generous with their wisdom. This doesn't have to be a Buddhist teacher; it can be anyone who has positively influenced your life. It can even be a grandparent who taught you valuable life lessons. Hold their image in mind, feeling your gratitude for their support.

3. Contemplating the Suffering of All Beings

The third practice would be to contemplate the great suffering of all beings. There is pain that we all go through as part of life and the idea is that when we turn our attention to that, we do not need to get overwhelmed, but allow this knowledge to rouse feelings of compassion and tenderness toward all beings.

If contemplating the suffering of *all* beings feels overwhelming to you, you can think of a specific group of people. It might be individuals you read about in the news who suffer in a war-torn area or people who are suffering in your own neighborhood. It doesn't even have to be people; it can be animals. It can be the beings in the cat shelter down the street from you. It can be that specific if you would like.

Meditation for Rousing Bodhichitta

I want to offer a guided meditation to connect with bodhichitta. As with our other meditations, you can listen to me guide you at lodrorinzler.com/youaregood. There is no getting this meditation wrong. Any tenderness or openness you may feel while contemplating these beings is the entire point of the thing. Whoever comes to mind is great. The point is to allow their images to serve as springboards into bodhichitta.

1. Find a comfortable meditation posture and connect to your breath, allowing it to flow naturally. If your mind wanders, gently bring it back to the breath.
2. After a few minutes, bring to mind the image of someone who has shown you great kindness and support. You don't have to do anything with this image; just visualize the person as if they are in the room with you. As you do, notice if your heart starts to soften in response. As in mindfulness meditation, when the mind starts to wander, we come back to the image, as we do in the breath practice. Stay with this image and let your heart soften toward this individual for a few minutes. If there is an aspiration that you would like to make for their well-being —"May you feel happy" or "May you know peace"— feel free to offer words that feel genuine to you. Then take a deep breath, letting the image go with the exhale.

3. Next, visualize a mentor or teacher who has provided you with wisdom. As before, we hold their image in mind as if they are with us. You can think of the way they do their hair, the way they smile, or even the way they dress; whatever allows you to viscerally feel the image is good. As you spend this time with them, soften your heart in gratitude for them. After a few minutes, if there is an aspiration that you would like to make for their well-being—"May you feel loved" or "May you experience joy"—feel free to offer words that feel authentic to you. Then take a deep breath, letting the image go with the exhale.
4. Finally, bring to mind a group of beings who are currently suffering in some way. It can be a family that you know that is going through hard times, or a group you read about online, or other individuals entirely. Hold them in your mind to the best of your ability. Even if you have only a vague sense of this group and cannot visualize each individual, that is fine. Notice if there is some tenderness in response to bringing these individuals to mind. It might feel a bit raw or uncomfortable. But we stay with them, as we did in the previous steps, letting ourselves feel that openness of heart while we spend this time with them. After a few minutes, you can once more make an aspiration—"May you feel safe" or "May you feel freedom"—or something else entirely. Then take a deep breath, letting them go with the exhale.

Notice how you feel. See if there is any openness or feeling of love, vulnerability, or tenderness. Rest there for a while. Then when you are done meditating, go do something nurturing for yourself.

14 YOUR KID IS BASICALLY GOOD

I'll start off by saying that most parents probably believe more in their kids' basic goodness than in their own. When we look in the mirror, we may see all our flaws and doubts staring back. But when we look into the face of a loved one, especially a child, there's often a direct experience of bodhichitta—that vulnerable, tender, and open-hearted awareness.

Even if you're still coming to terms with your own sense of basic goodness, I want to invite you to reflect on a young child you know. This may be your own kid or it might be a niece or nephew. It could be your godchild or your friend's kid whom you feel particularly close to. Take the time to bring their image to mind. Remember how they laugh and the color of their eyes. Close your own eyes for thirty seconds and just bring your full attention to that image.

Now that your eyes are open, how is your heart? If I had to guess, I'd say it is softer, more caring, and open. That is the amazing thing about kids, particularly the ones we feel close to. Their basic goodness is on full display, and we, in the act of witnessing it, are changed and cracked open by their presence. It's almost effortless to look into a child's eyes and see that they were born basically good. These kids in your life? They're firmly in the "people I like" camp.

Right before my own baby was born, I had a chance to talk with my Buddhist teacher, Kilung Rinpoche, about my meditation practice. For the previous four years, under his guidance, I had been dedicating a few weeks each year to meditation retreats, along with close to two hours of daily practice. But with a newborn on the way, I was worried that all this would soon be out of reach. "I don't think I'll be able to keep up with my practice and retreats the way I'd like. There's no way I can do that with a newborn," I said.

His words will forever be burned into my brain. He looked at me, genuinely surprised, and simply said, "Just be present for your child. Be attentive to baby."

Sometimes we foolish meditation practitioners get caught up in all sorts of concepts about what meditation *should* look like. We imagine a pristine environment, silent and serene, maybe with a lovely altar in front of us, and then—and only then—can we find some connection to our innate peace and calm.

That is simply not the case. I've been teaching meditation for over twenty years now and I can't count the number of times when a meditation student felt frustrated with their life and said that what they really wanted to do was escape to a monastery, to Tibet or Thailand, or to a cave in the woods. I'm all for solitude and setting aside dedicated time for practice, but in these conversations the implication is not "I am taking time to meditate." It's more "If only I could escape the confines of my daily life, then I would find peace."

Whenever this conversation occurs I tend to think about an old *Saturday Night Live* skit featuring Adam Sandler, who plays a tour guide in a commercial for trips to Italy. He lists all of the glorious things you can see on your vacation, and then toward the end issues a disclaimer: "But remember, you're still going to be you on vacation. If you are sad where you are, and then you get on a plane to Italy, the you in Italy will be the same sad you from before."

I love this point. Your mind is still your mind, whether you're at home juggling bills or sipping an Aperol Spritz in Italy. You are still you, no matter where you go.

Applying this principle to meditation: you could be on the most breathtaking mountaintop with the most beautiful sunset, like we see on the cover of yoga magazines, and mentally you could still be trapped at work, rehashing an argument, or fretting over finances. The environment has not changed our fixation. In other words, your meditation practice does not necessitate the perfect setting. Whether your child is being adorable or, let's face it, kind of annoying, your mind is your mind, your life is your life.

What I mean is that wherever you are, whatever situation you find yourself in, can *be* your meditation practice. You can meditate in a cramped apartment with construction going on outside, and that is an excellent opportunity to cultivate patience and compassion. You can practice while traveling on an overpacked flight as you bounce through turbulence, grounding yourself in the calm that exists within.

The breath is always available to us; we just need to remember to tune in to it. We always have an opportunity to be present.

Coming full circle to basic goodness, after that conversation with my teacher, I began engaging in something I call Newborn Meditation. My daughter would look me in the eyes, daring me to be fully present with her or to try to escape by staring at my phone or chasing some other distraction. In those moments, I had a choice: to see the baby as an interruption or to treat *her* as the practice itself. This is when my teacher's words echoed in my mind: "Be attentive to baby." I would set my practice text or work aside, look into her eyes, and ask, "What can I do for you, baby?" In my mind I was saying, "I am here for you. You are suffering? I will do what I can to help." In that moment, I was able to connect directly to both my basic goodness and hers.

Imagine if we brought this attitude into our interactions with everyone in our lives. "Be attentive to baby" becomes code for "Be present with whoever is in front of you." The person holding up the line, the family member caught up in drama, the friend in need. The practice becomes, "I am here for you. You are suffering? I will do what I can to help."

This is one of the many ways we can build the bridge from formal meditation practice on our cushion and our daily life. We don't have to separate out "This is my *real* meditation" and "This over here, this person in line or family member or friend is something else." We can merge them, accepting each person as an invitation to be present. In that moment, we realize that this too is practice. *Be attentive to baby.* Everyone is baby.

And when the "babies" in your life really push your buttons, it can actually be a good thing. There's an old story about the Buddhist master Atisha. Atisha was very wise and an excellent teacher, so he had been asked to travel from India to Tibet to offer Buddhist teachings there. But he had heard rumors that the Tibetan people were exceptionally nice. "That won't do," he thought. "If everyone is nice to me all the time, how will I grow spiritually?"

As a result, he decided to bring a Bengali tea servant with him. This guy was a mess. He was always dropping things and making the most inappropriate statements that tried Atisha's patience and compassion. "Yes," Atisha must have thought, "this is the person who is going to push my buttons; I'll bring him." He knew that without someone challenging him, he wouldn't be able to develop the qualities he wanted, like patience, kindness, and equanimity.

It's a bit like lifting weights. If I lifted the same twenty-five-pound dumbbell every single time I went to the gym, at a certain point it would stop being a challenge; my muscles would adapt and my training would become stagnant. It's only when I then pick up thirty- or thirty-five-pound weights that I would start to feel discomfort, and that's when growth occurs.

Spiritually, it's the same. Atisha was worried that if he surrounded himself with really nice people he would never be pushed outside his comfort zone and thus all the important qualities he wanted to cultivate—discipline, compassion, concentration, and the rest—would never be refined. He also knew that the best way to grow his spiritual muscles was to feel that discomfort. As the story goes, he brought his tea servant to Tibet only to find that the Tibetans weren't *quite* as nice as he'd heard. He actually had plenty of opportunities to get annoyed in their company and thus become patient and more open-hearted every day.

Similarly, when you have a young child, this being can delightfully test you, giving you ample chances to cultivate all of your good qualities. They are not particularly interested in your plans for the day. They want what they want and they are not shy about telling you. You might envision a peaceful afternoon at the museum and end up instead at the park. You think you can sneak in a few emails, but instead you're pulled into a game of tag. None of it feels completely at ease: it's unpredictable, and most of us don't love unpredictability. Yet this little "tea servant" is helping you grow spiritually.

I know that asking you to adopt this perspective might seem unusual. When you are on the fiftieth version of answering the child's eternal question, "Why?" you may feel like your patience has been tested enough for the day. In those moments, it's time to reconnect to the child's basic goodness, as well as your own. You are basically good. So are they. Can you recognize their inherent goodness, the peace underneath the current storm, and relate to them from that perspective?

I was raised Buddhist, so people often ask me what it was like growing up meditating. To be honest, I inwardly always chuckle at this question because it's not like I have a whole other childhood without meditation to compare it to. With that in mind, I shift the question into what I think is more potent territory: basic goodness.

My parents started practicing Buddhism in their twenties and were well-immersed in its principles by the time they had me in their early forties. At that point in their lives, they were already steeped in the culture of basic goodness. Whether intentional or not, they raised me with the belief that I was basically good. Again, I have no other childhood to compare it to, but I think this view of basic goodness is the thing that most affected me growing up.

With basic goodness permeating the household, when something went wrong, it did not mean *I* was bad or wrong. I was basically good and I had made a mistake. Those are two wildly different views to hold. The act of wiping boogers on the wall (yes, I was a gross child) did not make me a bad child. I was a basically good kid who needed to learn how to use tissues.

I imagine I was just as delightful and trying as any other kid my age, but my parents were unwavering in the commitment to seeing my basic goodness. This let me grow into adolescence and adulthood with a confidence in my basic wholeness that I don't think many of my peers possessed. When things didn't go my way, it wasn't because I was a failure. I was whole and enough as I was, and things just didn't go my way in that particular instance.

When parents ask me what it was like growing up meditating, I sometimes think that they are asking me because they want their kids to meditate, or if we're being honest, they want their kids to quickly experience the benefits of meditation and *calm down*. When I'm asked this question I always answer with a question for them: "Do you meditate?"

"No," they often reply, "but I really think my kid would benefit from it."

I will use this chance to point out that I am by no means a parenting expert, but in my limited experience and understanding I do know that kids pick up a lot by osmosis. They mirror what they see in their caregivers. I began meditating at the age of six only because I'd seen my parents doing it for years without making much of an issue about it. With that in mind, if you want your kid to meditate, then meditate.

Similarly, if you want your kids to grow up connected to and acting from a place of basic goodness, connect to your own and do your best to live your life through that lens. It will affect every relationship you have, but perhaps none more so than this child who is looking to you as a model for how to live their life.

The more you root yourself in your own basic goodness, the more you see others, especially children, through that lens. And the more you do that, the more they're inspired to relax into that same state of being. Yes, these little tea servants might test you, but they're daily reminders that basic goodness is real and accessible when we slow down and recognize it in others. We just have to be attentive to baby.

15 YOUR SPOUSE IS BASICALLY GOOD

My wife and I have been together, at the time of this writing, for over a decade. One thing I have discovered over that period of time is that we have a very different understanding of what a clean house looks like. For me, everything should have a place, and I'm less concerned about dog hair on the couch. For her, the couch absolutely has to be hair-free, but she's unbothered if there are dishes all around the house.

In theory, that would mean we both stick to our sweet spots and the house is clean all the time and everyone is happy. And yet we are a normal couple, and when I see multiple water glasses left in the living room, my mind can veer into annoyance and any feeling of bodhichitta—compassionate, openhearted awareness—momentarily fades.

To be clear, of the three categories of people mentioned earlier, my wife—and likely the person you may be seeing romantically—falls into that group of the people I like. My wife is wise and kind and beautiful and I'm incredibly lucky to have her in my life. Being with her is like being with a mirror for my own basic goodness, and she constantly awakens bodhichitta in me.

And yet, as in my experiences with kids, we can hold all of those truths and still mildly annoy each other.

Earlier we discussed the three root poisons in Buddhism—passion, aggression, and ignorance—that arise as part of our human experience. It's normal for these three to arise in daily life, and especially in the context of a romantic relationship. There are times when you feel quite passionate about this person that you share your life with, other times when you keep to yourselves and tune out the person down the hall, and occasionally times when you get frustrated or irritated with each other.

David Richo, a longtime therapist and author, discusses what helps relationships thrive in *How to Be an Adult in Relationships*. He describes the five A's that allow love to flourish: Attention, Acceptance, Appreciation, Affection, and Allowing.

The first *A*, Attention, often means cultivating the presence and mindfulness we've explored throughout this book. When I show up and give my wife my full attention, as I would my child, there is no room for resentment or frustration. I am simply there with her. By letting go of the stories I might tell myself about her or our relationship, I create the space to experience her basic goodness more directly, along with my own bodhichitta.

The second *A* is Acceptance. There was a moment, years ago, when I got down on one knee and asked my wife to marry me. In my complete intellectualization of marriage I thought, "Okay. I know this person well. I know what is great about them and I know some of their so-called weaknesses. Yes, I can accept and be in partnership with all of her, wholly and without reservation." Incidentally, how weird is it that in many cases the decision to marry involves one person making up their mind alone and then springing the question on the other person as a complete surprise? It's like saying, "I've taken my time and made up my mind to spend the rest of my life with you. Do you want to do that? Answer 'yes' or 'no' right now please!" Mercifully, Adreanna said yes. From there, we navigated the logistics of what marriage meant to each of us as we moved toward a wedding day. There were a lot of honest conversations about what we wanted from the relationship and acknowledgments of differences that we would have to become okay with from now on.

Yet simply being okay with the eccentricities of another person for the rest of your life is easily said but harder to do. One question I often come back to: How quickly can I let go of the stories that keep me locked in pain and come back to recognizing this person's basic goodness? In other words, it's okay to feel annoyed when glasses are stacked in the living room, but can I notice the feeling and just pick them up without letting frustration spiral into a story that amplifies the irritation? That's where the training in mindfulness meditation really shines.

The third *A* is Appreciation. It's only in the last year or two that my wife and I have leaned into the simple power of saying the appreciative thing we might think in our own heads aloud to the other person in a regular and consistent manner. It's sort of a game changer. This could be saying out loud how good the other looks in their outfit, admiring how great they are with the kid, or anything else that spontaneously comes to mind.

Any time one of us cooks, there is a moment of genuine gratitude. It's not, "Oh yeah; I should say 'thank you.'" Knowing how busy we both are, it's a real acknowledgment: "Thank you for doing this so I can tend to other parts of our life together."

Then there is the fourth *A*, Affection. Not to mix methodologies, but my wife's love language is touch. I wasn't raised in a particularly physically affectionate household, so it took me until this relationship to really understand how powerful a long hug can be. I recently read that Disney World has a hug rule for its characters: they're not supposed to let go first when hugging a child; the child can hug as long as they want. The idea behind it is that you never know how much a child may need that hug, which just breaks my heart wide open. My wife and child don't know this, but I've adopted that approach in our own home.

The fifth *A* is Allowing, which comes down to letting your partner be who they genuinely are and to do things they love to do. Adreanna is surprisingly tolerant of the X-Men podcast I run. I only really know about two things in life: Buddhism and X-Men, and running my silly podcast scratches an itch deep inside me, and she gets that. Meanwhile, while I am working on this chapter today, Adreanna is at a garlic festival. Sure, I get the bizarre appeal of a festival devoted entirely to garlic and am happy to watch the kid so she can enjoy it.

Sometimes we lose sight of our partner's basic goodness because we've built up so many fixed ideas about who we think they are. We take this vibrant, garlic-loving person and wrap them tight in layers of our own assumptions. As a result, it's not, "It looks like my wife may have left out a water glass," but, "She *always* leaves glasses around the house, this is just who she is." When we use words like "always" or "never," we are boxing this person into one solid consistent idea of who we perceive them to be.

In other words, when you look at your partner, it's your idea of your partner that you are seeing. No one has that set group of ideas but you. Their mother, for instance, has a different set of stories that she has solidified about who this person is. Similarly your partner's best friend has a different set of ideas. This is the nature of how we all cover over the true identity of our loved ones with stories we ourselves come up with day after day, year after year. We tell ourselves things like: "My partner is generous with her time. My partner is bad with money. My partner is the better singer." All of these are ideas we have hatched along the way and reified to come up with a simplistic notion of who we believe them to be.

My wife introduced me to the following framework (again, she is quite wise). The approach I just mentioned is generally considered looking at the relationship as a lawyer rather than as a scientist. The lawyer approach is going about our day looking for ways to continue to prop up our idea about something and building a case to support that idea, often ignoring contradictory data that doesn't support our vision. When I see a water glass out in the open, that is another notch supporting my idea of who my wife is . . . until I realize that I left it there myself.

Looking at a relationship as a scientist, however, means approaching what is going on with fresh eyes and a curious mind. When you were first getting to know your person, I imagine you had boundless curiosity about them. You wanted to know their favorite movies, their favorite foods, what music they listened to, and more. Then, once you checked off those boxes of desired information, you settled into the idea that you truly know this person.

Yet if someone asked you about your favorite movies, foods, and music now versus five years ago, wouldn't you come up with somewhat different answers? I imagine the answer is yes. So we know that these things can change, yet we forget that our partner too is changing. Because of our forgetfulness, we fail to reinvest the time and energy it takes to learn all about who our spouse has become today.

The greatest gift we can offer our partner is our understanding. I am using the word *understanding* intentionally here, in the sense that we seek to understand who they currently are as opposed to getting lost in our idea of who we believe them to be. Understanding requires two things from us: presence and curiosity.

Presence

Sometimes I feel that I state very obvious things, but here is one of them: we need to be fully present with our partner. Going back to the first *A* of attention, this often means putting away our phones and other distractions so that we can limit the number of ways we get pulled away from the present moment. This might look like a quiet dinner for just the two of you or taking a walk together. You create the space to just fully be there with your loved one.

The Vietnamese Zen master Thich Nhat Hanh came up with four mantras for true presence. He said,

> The greatest gift we can make to others is our true presence. 'I am here for you' is a mantra to be uttered in perfect concentration. When you are concentrated—mind and body together—you produce your true presence, and anything you say is a mantra. It does not have to be in Sanskrit or Tibetan. A mantra can be spoken in your own language: 'Darling, I am here for you.'[1]

"Darling, I am here for you" is the first mantra. It denotes that we are bringing our full self, our basically good self, to this person right in front of us.

"I know you are there, and I am very happy" is the second mantra. Here we are acknowledging the presence of the other person and the joy that this connection can bring us.

"Darling, I know you suffer. That is why I am here for you" is the third mantra. We are acknowledging that there are so many aches and pains that take place in this life and that we yearn to provide support to this other person.

The fourth is said to be the most difficult: "Darling, I suffer. Please help." The reason this is difficult is because we often carry too much pride to admit that we ourselves are in pain and that this person who loves us could be of support. Yet Thich Nhat Hanh has said, "In true love, there is no place for pride."[2]

As simple as it sounds, we need to be fully present with our partner. This means putting away distractions and showing up entirely, perhaps during a quiet dinner or a walk together. By doing so, we create the space to truly be there with them.

Curiosity

With true presence, curiosity comes naturally. This is a manifestation of a connection to our own basic goodness. We are delighted by the present moment and are now very interested in it. If we are with our spouse, that means we might naturally begin to ask questions about them.

A powerful question to ask might be, "Who are you today?" They might respond with, "I am an overwhelmed person," or "I am someone who is obsessed with this new show I'm watching," or "I am someone mourning a past version of myself." This question is simply an invitation for someone to consider what is coming up for them in a given moment that we are sharing together.

If that question feels too formal to you, almost anything other than "How was your day?" will do. Any question that shifts the habitual dynamic between you two from "the same old" to "this is new" is delightful.

We as humans like to talk about ourselves, so this is not a particularly challenging thing to do, to ask a few questions. Yet the moment we start, we may find there are infinite new things to talk about: What podcast is this person listening to? Which friends are they connecting to these days? What is inspiring them and what new things have they learned?

All of a sudden, we may find some of our old ideas about this person falling away. We may discover we are in a relationship with someone very different from who we thought they were and be surprised by it. Because their conglomeration of knowledge and experience is shifting constantly, we don't have to settle into an idea of "now *this* is who this person is" but can continue to explore the topic week after week, year after year, seeing how this person is changing.

When presence and curiosity come together, they lead to genuine understanding. We now understand who this person is because we see them with fresh eyes. We experience them as who they are, not who they were when we first started dating. We experience them in their fullness, and in that moment, bodhichitta—the open heart—dawns.

This experience of more deeply understanding the person we spend all this time with allows us to recognize their basic goodness more readily. We then reconnect to our open, tender heart. All of a sudden, this person isn't someone who is purposefully inconsiderate and didn't do what you asked them to do. They are basically good and kind and wise, and likely didn't remember to do that thing you asked. These are subtle distinctions I am making, but taking the view of "this person is amazing as they are and made a mistake" is very different from "this person is an inconsiderate jerk."

The more we can get present and curious about our partner, the more quickly we drop our petty annoyances and connect to the basic goodness of this person we cherish. We discover that they are basically good, we are basically good, and from there we can move forward together.

16 STRANGERS ARE BASICALLY GOOD

I'm going to say something that sounds a little mean. It's not about you specifically, it's about all of us: we're all a little self-involved. We tend to see ourselves as the main character in the story of our lives, and because of this, most people we encounter become supporting cast—extras who fill minor roles in the movie of our day-to-day lives. They play the cashier we chat with for thirty seconds or the police officer we nod to while walking down the street. They are the nameless patrons of the restaurant we eat at and the people in line ahead of us at the supermarket. We have a tendency to forget that those same people are also walking around with main-character energy and that we are the extras in their movies.

Some of the practices we have explored, such as loving-kindness, have a remarkable ability to strip us of our self-involvement and help us see the people around us more clearly. As in the presence and curiosity we brought to our relationship with our spouse, we can begin to seek to truly understand everyone else we encounter in the environment around us.

The Irish poet William Butler Yeats is often attributed with the quote, "There are no strangers here, only friends you haven't yet met." When my wife and I moved to a small village in upstate New York with a population of twelve hundred, I took that idea to heart. There are no strangers where we live, just neighbors and potential friends we likely will, at some point in the future, have some type of relationship with. Now we may not literally befriend every stranger we encounter, but I came to the conclusion that we at least ought to acknowledge their basic goodness, welcoming them as friends in our own minds and hearts.

At this point in our spiritual journey, we're shifting from our comfort zone of the "people I like" to include "everyone else"—that is, the people we often ignore. They are sometimes referred to as neutral people. If passion or attachment is the root poison most associated with the "people I like" group, here we are now working with the root poison of ignorance—often translated from Sanskrit as "prejudice"—when relating to these strangers.

"Prejudice" is an interesting term in our Western parlance, in that we all possess unconscious biases. For example, if you grew up with stereotypes about people who look a certain way or believe in particular things, even if you've never personally experienced what those stereotypes suggest, you may notice a subtle reaction every time you encounter someone who fits that image. Or it might be simpler, like the memory of a high-school bully. Maybe you meet someone who reminds you of that person, and you reflexively pull back, no matter how kind they may be. These unconscious biases are often a standard part of the human experience.

In the same way that meditation can help us unlearn other nonhelpful patterns and behavior, it can aid us in the quest to undo our biases and unlearn whatever prejudices we may have developed. From a Buddhist perspective, we are not inherently prejudiced people, we are basically good. One way to consider prejudice is that it is ignorance of a situation that is then hardened into learned behavior. The good news is that because it is learned, it can also be unlearned.

There are countless more eloquent books on how to unlearn biases, so I will leave that topic here. But I encourage each of us to do our inner work of looking directly at what we are actively ignoring in our own relationship to the world around us. It is when we begin to become curious about our ignorance and shine a light on it that the darkness evaporates and we let go of patterns that no longer serve us.

When Buddhists use the terms "ignorance" and "prejudice," they mean that we are *actively* or *intentionally* ignoring what the reality of a given situation may be. For example, when I am at the post office lost in thought, I most likely will actively ignore the other conversations happening around me, the people coming and going, and the postal employees themselves, until I am called to the front of the line. In this instance I have actively chosen to place my attention on me and my concerns over relating to the world around me. That is the type of ignorance we are discussing in this context.

Because we are so me-centric, we lose sight of reality as it is. It's like looking at a piece of art. If you push your eye up against the framed piece you might say with some definitiveness, "This painting is about the color orange!" Then once you take a step back, you may realize that what you were looking at was but one small part of a jacket and think, "This is a painting of an orange jacket!" Then when you take several more steps back, you see that in fact the painting is of a group of people, one of whom happens to be wearing an orange jacket.

This is often how we experience life. We are so focused on our small corner of the painting that we lack the ability to understand the greater whole. When we begin meditating, we begin to realize that the world does not revolve around us. We take a small step back from focusing just on the me part of the painting, noticing all the other neutral people around us. We are but extras in everyone else's movies—one person wearing an orange jacket in a crowd—and that's okay! This is the access point to realizing that we are interconnected in many ways, in particular in our shared basic goodness.

Sometimes when I am driving, I find myself marveling at how many neutral people surround me. There are drivers in nearby cars, people in houses I pass by, cyclists on bikes cruising the street, and more. Even though I'm driving alone, I'm surrounded by a larger community.

The other day, I found myself behind a white Jeep. Inside was a man, perhaps about ten years older than me, and his small dog who was joyfully hanging its head out the passenger-side window. At first, this was a neutral situation for me. They were in their car, I was in mine, and so I figured I could probably ignore them. I was focused instead on what I wanted to listen to and where I was going and what I would do when I got there.

But neutrality can shift in an instant. Suddenly, the Jeep slowed to ten miles under the speed limit—and I had a haircut to get to. All of a sudden, the neutral situation turned negative: I don't like this thing. I don't like this thing because I have sorted this man into the mental group of people who are inconsiderate of those around them—"people I don't like"—and he will make me late and I don't like being late, so now I've decided I don't like this man.

Recently, I've been trying to see the world with fresh eyes, partly because of how my daughter is experiencing everything for the first time. The Zen master Suzuki Roshi put it best when he encouraged us to view the world through "beginner's mind"—a mind that is open to things exactly as they are, seeing every aspect of the world as a beginner would.

Maybe because I was practicing this, I noticed my habitual reaction and paused. The man looked happy and was bopping around in his seat. As if he was listening to what he wanted to listen to. The dog was visibly overjoyed to be along for the ride. This was perhaps a rare moment for the two of them. At that moment I thought, "How foolish of me to forget how rare all of this is." There is a morbid joke I recalled upon seeing the two of them together: a man goes to see a fortune teller, who tells him that in a dozen years he will face heartbreaking loss. In order to cheer himself up, on the way home he adopts a puppy.

I smiled for this man, recognizing the basic goodness of this complete stranger and his dog, and slowed down, giving them space on the road so they didn't feel rushed by me. I could afford to be late. I was busy taking joy in their joy, a man and his dog out for a ride. It didn't matter whether they recognized the fleeting nature of this happiness; they were present to it and so was I. By sharing in their happiness, my frustration melted and I felt more connected to my own basic goodness.

To help us shift our focus from just ourselves to the world around us, we can adapt our mindfulness meditation to include a broader awareness of the environment. This meditation technique is sometimes called mindfulness-awareness practice. It is like taking a few steps back from the painting. It involves balancing our focus on the breath with a gentle awareness of everything we perceive around us through our senses, allowing us to open to the world as a whole.

Mindfulness-Awareness Meditation

This meditation can also be found as an audio recording at lodrorinzler.com/youaregood. To begin, take your "good" meditation posture, the posture that allows you to feel relaxed yet uplifted. Connect to the natural sensation of the breath. Allow yourself to enjoy each in-breath and out-breath as they move through you.

When you notice that you have drifted off into thought, gently come back to feeling each breath. If it's helpful, label the thought "thinking" very kindly and then return to the present.

After a few minutes, I recommend you change the technique very slightly. You can begin to keep approximately a quarter of your attention on your breath while allowing the other three-quarters to enter into the environment. Simply relax your sense perceptions and allow them to take in whatever is occurring in the present moment, right alongside the breath.

One way to get used to this particular style of meditation is to begin by noticing what you hear. We often block out simple sensations because we are so lost in our own heads. You might notice the sounds of loved ones nearby, the refrigerator humming, or cars passing in the street. You might hear the internal sounds of your body doing its routine maintenance. Just notice what you hear while also staying attuned to each breath.

When you are ready, you can begin to notice what you smell, see, taste, and touch. Are scents of candles or flowers present? If your eyes are open, take in the grain of the wood or the color of the carpet ahead of you. Nothing is being ignored here, you are simply being present to your environment and your breath.

As thoughts pull you away from your experience of the present moment, gently acknowledge them as before—"thinking"—and come back to the breath, opening up to the environment around you when you are once again ready to do so.

Take ten or fifteen minutes for this practice, then transition out of the meditation at your own pace. Continue to see whether you can remain open to the environment in your post-meditation hours and whether you are more present to the activities and, most important, the people around you than you previously were.

Those people we might label "everyone else" and normally ignore? Try to notice them, bringing a sense of presence to each encounter. By simply being present, we can recognize their basic goodness. When we're fully aware in the moment, we're more likely to see these strangers for who they truly are, recognize their inherent nature, and perhaps even smile in acknowledgment.

17 YOUR EX IS BASICALLY GOOD

Of the three groups I mentioned earlier, I have saved the juiciest for last: those individuals we label the "people I don't like."

I hope that for you this is a small camp made up of only a few people. In traditional Buddhist texts, individuals in this group are sometimes referred to as enemies. Assuming you do not have an archnemesis, like Spider-Man's Green Goblin, then this group is likely made up of people who have pissed you off or wronged you in some way.

The Buddhist view is that everyone possesses basic goodness, including those in the "people I don't like" camp. This means your ex, your jerk of a co-worker, your racist uncle . . . everyone is basically good . . . and yes, at the same time, we can acknowledge that they at times act out in confused and hurtful ways.

In today's world, it seems increasingly difficult for many of us to hold opposing points of view at once. All too often people want to be right and to find someone who believes something they do not and make that person wrong. Here I am asking you to fight the tendency to want to solidify the notions of "good" and "bad" people and to instead look at the people we have a hard time with as basically good *and* also deeply confused. We have to hold both perspectives in our minds.

In order to get there, we can reflect on the times we ourselves made mistakes or were in the wrong, and how that does not erase our own basic goodness. Have you ever made a mistake? I have—when I felt disconnected from my basic goodness and as a result acted in deeply confused ways. This isn't even a "before I started meditating" kind of story. Remember, I started meditating when I was six.

The other night my wife asked an interesting question: "At what point do we allow people to change?" She was pointing out how we often grant ourselves leeway in recognizing that we are not the same people we were five or ten years ago. Yet when it comes to the perceived wrongdoing of others, we tend to fix that in our minds: "This is who this person is."

I spent many years in confusion, inadvertently causing harm due to that confusion. There was a period in my late twenties, after my father died, when I was overworked and adrift in a thousand different emotions. During that time, I drank too much, made poor decisions, and often caused myself pain, sometimes even hurting other people. At least one of them continues to feel harmed by me today, and I carry a deep sense of regret about that. I did what I could do to mend the situation—I sought mediation and apologized—but some things aren't easily fixed.

Through therapy, counseling with mentors, and conversations with my wife over the years, I've turned over every potential rock regarding the harm I caused in my twenties and sought to learn from it. However, in doing inner work there comes a point where you can't keep turning over the same rocks. I've reflected on the moments I have caused harm in my past countless times, considering them from as many perspectives as possible.

At some point I had to make a personal decision to acknowledge that I have learned and sought to make amends with those I hurt, and then, dedicated to not repeating the harmful behavior, I moved forward in a new direction. In spending years contemplating past actions, I came to know myself and others much better and could recommit to causing the least possible harm for the remainder of my lifetime. At some point there's only so far you can go with a given issue when you're dedicated to not repeating it.

Returning to my wife's question: "At what point do we allow people to change?" I know I am not the same version of Lodro that existed a dozen years ago. Since then, I've done my best to make up for my past actions. None of them means I'm not basically good. I am basically good and was grieving and having a really hard time, acting out of confusion. I can hold both truths in my mind, and I hope you can too.

I mention this because I think it's good for us to be honest about the times we ourselves may have ended up in someone's "people I don't like" camp. We all have moments when we felt disconnected from our basic goodness, acted in confusion, and harmed ourselves and others. I don't know your specific circumstances, yet I can say that pretty definitively because *we have all done it.*

Okay, fine. You and I have acted out of confusion due to a disconnect from our basic goodness. That's forgivable. But what about the difficult people in your life? You might be thinking, "No, Lodro. You don't understand. My ex is the devil incarnate. There is no goodness there to connect to."

Earlier when we discussed finding the basic goodness in your spouse, I mentioned that when you look at them it's your idea of them that you see. In many relationships, whether they are doing well or going sour, at a certain point these ideas harden into set versions of who we believe this person to be. We see this person as a caricature of who they are. When that happens, it becomes much easier to write off the nuances of their character and simply say "They are bad." This kind of definitive statement—"There is no goodness there"—is not just flippant; it negates their humanity.

When we deny someone the potential to wake up to their basic goodness, we reduce them to something less than human. All humans have basic goodness and the ability to wake up to it. Some of us just have a harder road to get there than others.

When we say, "This person is bad," we ourselves have made a choice to close our hearts off to them. At one point, you loved your ex, for example. There was so much intimacy and care. Then, perhaps seemingly out of nowhere, you broke up. They cheated on you, or you got tired of their behavior, or something else happened entirely. In that moment you went from being open-hearted with them all the time to intentionally shutting down your heart.

I understand that this is a pretty typical defense mechanism, and I don't fault you for kicking your ex out of your heart. However, the more you tend to your healing, the more you may find there is room to reconnect to your own basic goodness and to have the capacity to understand them better, ultimately recognizing their goodness as well. This is when bodhichitta is reactivated—when we seek to understand another person.

There is a fine line I want to draw in the sand between barriers and boundaries when it comes to the heart. Do me a favor. Place your hands up in front of your face with your fingers pressed tightly together. It is very hard to see and connect to the world when we have such a barrier in place, no? Now let the fingers spread apart. There is still some obstruction but we can see the world around us a bit more clearly. This illustrates the distinction between a barrier and a boundary.

A barrier is this negation of humanity, a strong "I refuse to acknowledge that this person has the potential to drop their confusion and become a better person." We may never see this person again, and so that hardening of the heart only hurts ourselves. We walk around with a little icebox where our warm and tender heart used to be, and that is really very painful for us.

Meanwhile, a boundary in this context is a sense that we can keep our heart open to them, even if we aren't welcoming them back with open arms. We can, even from the safety of our own homes, wish this person well. We can hope that they are healing and taking good care of themselves, and that these activities help them reconnect to their basic goodness. We don't have to contact them or anything like that; this is simply about us opening our heart to them. I am advocating for some basic curiosity about this person, having simple moments where we think of them, opening our hearts and reconnecting with our bodhichitta to cultivate warmth and health.

It's impossible to underestimate how painful it is for all parties involved when we cut another person out of our hearts and negate their humanity, giving up on their basic goodness. It is easy to say, "That person is bad." It is much harder to say, "That person is suffering." No one acts like a jerk because everything is going well for them and they feel great about themselves. Harmful behavior comes from a place of pain.

When we look at the individuals in our "people I don't like" group, including our ex, we can say, "I see you. You are in pain. I am sorry for your suffering." This is an act that rouses our bodhichitta and reconnects us to our basic goodness. To acknowledge the suffering of your ex or other people you dislike is a true practice that brings about opportunities for healing and change.

18 WHAT ABOUT THAT WORLD-THREATENING POLITICIAN?

I've been teaching on the topic of basic goodness for over twenty years now, and in any perceptive audience there is always one question that will inevitably get asked once I've asserted that *everyone* has basic goodness: "What about Hitler?"

For much of my teaching career, "What about Hitler?" was the gold standard for this inquiry. Then starting in 2015 people began to ask, "What about Trump? And by 2022, "What about Putin?" It seems that in the past decade we have more readily accepted that there are certain individuals who can be considered irredeemable, devoid of basic goodness.

The short answer is "Yes, even Hitler." I need to pause before going on to the longer answer, which is that everyone is born with basic goodness. Hitler did atrocious things—crimes against humanity. I am not saying he is a good person or someone worth admiring. Quite the opposite. He was someone who was so distanced from his basic goodness that he was able to convince himself to do horrible things and that they were right, when clearly they were not.

Hitler did not emerge from the womb hating Jews. He learned that type of thinking over time, and that hate distanced him from any semblance of basic goodness. The consequences were catastrophic, resulting in the loss of entire branches of my family tree, as is the case for so many others.

It's hard to ask people to contemplate that even an authoritarian ruler or politician possesses basic goodness; it's a difficult topic for me as well. However, Trump and Putin, like anyone, have people they love who love them back, and they likely experience moments of genuine open-heartedness with those individuals. Someone right now—maybe you—likely hates that I'm using Trump as an example of basic goodness, but it's the one people have frequently mentioned to me, which is why I mention it here. Feel free to swap in a different ruling figure—Stalin, Mussolini, Pol Pot, Saddam Hussein, or others—as the point is the same. Even that person who you may tend to label "evil" is basically good . . . and not in touch with their innate goodness.

The Tibetan Buddhist teacher Chögyam Trungpa Rinpoche once famously said, "Everybody loves something. Even if it's just tortillas." This notion underscores a fundamental truth: everyone has the ability to soften and connect to the world around them, even if it's in very small ways. This is considered evidence that everyone—absolutely everyone—possesses basic goodness. Everyone is capable of love and compassion. There are no exceptions to this rule, no matter how confused an individual they may be or how distanced they currently are from their basic goodness.

19 THE DANGER OF VILLAINIZATION

When talking about the neutral people in our lives, I mentioned that we go through the world with main-character energy, considering people we don't know as extras in the movie of our life. And what would a movie be without at least one villain?

It's not uncommon for us to label someone a villain and then to start thinking like a lawyer, leveraging every new piece of information about them to prop up our case that they are a bad person. When information runs counter to our case—that they volunteer their time or that they are generous with their money, for example—we discount it by rationalizing that they are really doing it for selfish gain, which serves to reinforce our view of them as the bad guy.

Here is the interesting thing about putting someone in your "people I dislike" group: it doesn't help anyone. It doesn't help you. You do not benefit from hardening your heart and labeling that person as difficult. It doesn't help them. They do not benefit from you treating them like a difficult person. And it doesn't help other people. They do not benefit when you go around talking about what a horrible villain they are. Literally no one gains anything from this cycle.

Many times when people ask me about the difficult people in their lives, I ask them about how much time they have spent contemplating the humanity of their villain. When I bring up the old saying that "hurt people hurt people," I begin to see a dawning of recognition. When provoked, they acknowledge that it's possible that these "bad guys" are not acting from their best selves; in fact, they are likely acting from pain and hurt. In other words, they are disconnected from their basic goodness and act out of that disconnection in ways that hurt others.

Furthermore, when pressed, people who ask me about the basic goodness of their difficult people admit that they, too, have acted carelessly or harmfully when they were hurt or confused. Because, again, we have all done that at some point. In that sense, we're not completely different from these "villains."

No one wants to lead a life marked by hate. And yet this path of villainization leads us directly to that. When we lock someone out of our heart and label them unilaterally wrong or bad, then we are shutting ourselves off from a life marked by love.

I understand this intimately because I have been on both sides of it. I have labeled people villains in my own mind and began building a case against them. I have also been labeled a villain by others and have had every act I engage in viewed through that lens as well. I've been defamed online, and people who don't know me at all have said some of the most hateful things a person could say about me. Is what they say true? Not really! Does it still hurt? Absolutely.

The unfortunate thing is that other people read those words and are spooked by them. In one instance, I applied to be on the board of my local library. It's not a paid gig. It's not even one with any status. It's a volunteer position I put myself up for, motivated by my daughter's love for the library. I wanted to help them raise money so she could have a great space to go to growing up. But someone on the board came across negative things said about me, and I was deemed a liability and asked to step back from the role.

In both cases—me villainizing others or others villainizing me—all that happens is pain. It helps no one. In fact, in the library example, it just meant I couldn't volunteer to help my community. To reduce pain in this world, we have to let go of the hate in our hearts and seek to understand others.

With that in mind, here is my question for you: Have you ever been wrong about someone? I have. You hear something negative about a person and then go on their social media and think, "What a jerk! I can't believe how arrogant/ignorant/selfish they are." Then later we find out that the rumor is not entirely true and we think, "Oh. I guess I may have been wrong about them." This is a moment when we can continue to reinforce our villainizing narrative or we can begin to interrupt the flow of toxicity and aim to see them in a fresh light.

Not long ago, someone emailed me, angry about the trans-friendly language I used in a newsletter. This person revealed themselves to hold more conservative views than I do and called such language "insane," admonishing me to "protect" my daughter from it and this "trans fad." Initially, I was heartbroken that this person felt such hatred in her heart. But then something interesting happened: I got angry at her. I noticed stories well up and a desire to see this person's social media presence so that I might build a case about what a bigot they are. I was so ready to villainize this person over one email they sent me.

Then I remembered something the author Brené Brown once wrote: "People are hard to hate close up." I imagined what it would be like to ask this person for a phone conversation, just to get to know each other. I would not aim to change her mind about what I perceive to be her closed-mindedness but simply to connect. I imagined that in the span of ten minutes we would see a lot of similar interests, concerns, and desires for our own and others' well-being. To get up close to this person and realize that they are simply a suffering human—just like you and me—would cut through all of my anger and animosity. Even taking a few moments to engage in such a contemplation calmed me down and allowed me to access my bodhichitta.

One of my favorite quotes is from Representative John Lewis shortly before he passed away. In recounting the work he did in the early civil rights era he said, "We, from time to time, would discuss if you see someone attacking you, beating you, spitting on you, you have to think of that person—years ago, that person was an innocent child, innocent little baby. And so what happened? Something go wrong? Did the environment? Did someone teach that person to hate, to abuse others? So you try to appeal to the goodness of every human being. And you don't give up. You never give up on anyone."[1]

Here Representative Lewis was saying that even when someone attacks you and denigrates your humanity you could consider how they arrived at such a hardened state. What went wrong in this person's life that they closed off their heart so completely to other people? Who taught them how to hate so vehemently?

We can come back to the fundamental teachings on seeking to understand these types of people. When we do, we come to discover the basic goodness even in the people we would normally label as monsters. If we struggle and fail to find goodness in them, that is on us. It is there, and we need to keep letting go of our fixed ideas and opinions about them, becoming like scientists and opening our hearts wider. Everyone has something they love, some way of connecting with the world—it is up to us to discover it.

In doing so, even those who seem beyond redemption become recognizable as humans, capable of love and change. And we allow ourselves to stay open to the possibility of connection, love, and healing, never having to give up on anyone.

Loving-Kindness Meditation

Earlier I introduced the practice of loving-kindness, focusing specifically on offering it to various parts of yourself. Here I will introduce the full loving-kindness practice to deal with how we normally sort people into the categories of like, dislike, and ignore. Loving-kindness meditation allows us to slice through that duality to the extent that we can offer our bodhichitta to everyone, even the people we might begin to label "villain."

This meditation can also be found as an audio recording at lodrorinzler.com/youaregood. I recommend beginning this practice by practicing mindfulness meditation for a few minutes.

When you feel grounded, bring to mind an image of yourself. It could be how you appeared when you last saw your own reflection. It could be you as you appeared as a young child. Whatever feels most comfortable, bring that visualization to mind.

Touch in with your heart center. Let your heart soften. Repeat these words either in your own head or out loud in a tone just above a whisper:

May I feel happy

May I feel healthy

May I feel safe

May I feel peaceful

You can repeat these phrases three or more times, taking a moment in between to let the aspirations simply land in your being. Take a deep breath, and then you can let go of that image.

Now bring to mind someone in your life whom you consider easy to love. This is someone from the "people I like" group. It might be a friend, a dear family member, or perhaps even a romantic partner. We will make the same aspirations for them:

May you feel happy

May you feel healthy

May you feel safe

May you feel peaceful

As before, repeat those phrases three or more times. Then take another deep breath, letting go of this image of your loved one on the exhale.

Now bring to mind an image of someone you don't know very well. This is the "extra" in the movie of your life, someone whom you feel neutral about. We don't often consider this stranger in our day-to-day lives, but here we open our hearts to them and make the same aspiration:

May you feel happy

May you feel healthy

May you feel safe

May you feel peaceful

Repeat those phrases three times and then take a breath, letting the image go.

We now move into trickier territory: we bring to mind that person we find quite difficult, that "villain." This could be an ex, or a boss or client, or even a friend who you happen to be butting heads with right now.

Know that this person too just longs for happiness. Not unlike yourself, they are basically good and they sometimes act out of confusion. You can make the same aspiration for them:

May you feel happy

May you feel healthy

May you feel safe

May you feel peaceful

Repeat those phrases three or more times. At this point, you can bring everyone you have contemplated together: you, your loved one, this person you don't know very well, and this difficult person.

Here is an incredibly important step: we dissolve the boundaries of me versus you as we hold all of the previous people in mind. It becomes us:

May we feel happy

May we feel healthy

May we feel safe

May we feel peaceful

Breathing deeply, you can let these images go. Come back to noticing how your heart feels. Perhaps it feels raw, vulnerable, or tender.

Imagine your open heart, your bodhichitta, radiating love out from your entire body, not unlike the sun shining its rays in all directions. Your love shines 360 degrees from every pore of your skin. Your love reaches out and touches all beings everywhere.

We close with the aspiration:

May all beings feel happy

May all beings feel healthy

May all beings feel safe

May all beings feel peaceful

Let the images go. Just rest with any feeling of love and tenderness.

20 THE TWO WINGS OF A BIRD

The Vietnamese Zen master Thich Nhat Hanh was fond of saying, "In Buddhism we learn that understanding is the very foundation of love. If understanding is not there, no matter how hard you try, you cannot love."[1] Like the two wings a bird needs to fly, to become more in touch with our own basic goodness we also need two things: understanding and love.

We have looked at the people we like, the people we dislike, and everyone else with the sincere desire to learn to understand and love them more deeply. This journey is known in Buddhism as the birth of compassion.

The Sanskrit terms *prajna* and *karuna* are often translated as "understanding" and "love." Some Buddhist teachers would say those two wings of the bird are better translated as "wisdom" and "compassion," respectively. Here, prajna, or wisdom, is not about accumulating knowledge but about meeting reality where it is. It is the wisdom of seeing things for what they are, as opposed to viewing the world through our fixed expectations and biases. A commonly misunderstood Buddhist term that is linked with this concept is "emptiness."

If we want to truly understand reality for what it is, as opposed to being deluded by our confusion, we need to empty ourselves of our preconceptions and biases. We need to let go of all of the stories we tell ourselves about how things used to be or what they ought to be. Once we have let go of all that, we can see the world clearly. That is wisdom in the Buddhist tradition.

Earlier we talked about the four immeasurables, the four ways of offering limitless love: loving-kindness, compassion, sympathetic joy, and equanimity. We have covered loving-kindness in depth and now we can focus on compassion. The etymology of the word means "to feel with." It is not to pity another person or to consider them as below you spiritually. It is to bear witness to what they are experiencing. It is to feel what they are feeling. Compassion is based in being side by side with another person and seeking to understand what that person is going through.

Emptiness and compassion go together like the two wings of a bird because compassion requires a letting go or emptying out of our judgments and preconceived ideas about what someone might need from us. When we let go of what we think should happen for someone, we end up with an ability to meet the other person where they are. In other words, we need to fully understand someone else and their situation in order to best help them from a place of love.

When I first started dating my wife, she would sometimes bring me issues she was facing and, out of love for her, I would try to problem-solve them away. It took me a good amount of time to realize that what was really being asked of me was to let go of my problem-solving tendencies, bear witness to her suffering, and be there 100 percent with her. She did not need me to *do* anything. She needed me to *be* with her.

As I mentioned, in Sanskrit the word for compassion is *karuna*, which expresses a sincere desire to relieve the suffering of others. When we begin to meditate in earnest, we start to see more intimately the ways that we suffer. That increased awareness of our own pain leads us to raise our gaze, look around, and realize, "Oh yeah. Everyone else is suffering too. I need to be kind."

I can't emphasize how important this moment of realization is on someone's spiritual path. I have been teaching meditation for over twenty years and I am no stranger to the fact that most people get into the practice for personal reasons. People start because they want to be more at peace or less anxious. They want to feel more present or relaxed. And that's okay!

Yet at a certain point we see the bigger picture. We begin to acknowledge that this world we live in is not just about us. It's a bit like that moment in *The Matrix* when our hero, Neo, is offered two pills. If he takes the blue pill, he will wake up in his own bed and it will be as if what he has seen thus far was all a dream. Alternatively, if he takes the red pill he will remember everything and come to see how messed up his reality is.

Meditation is like taking the red pill. You can no longer avoid the fact that, yes, there is real suffering in your own life, but also that literally every other single being out there is also going through their own shit.

The good news is that meditation is a tool to help us get to know and befriend all of who we are, which is key in reconnecting to our basic goodness. Once we've let go of some of the barriers around our hearts, we are more able to skillfully help others do the same thing. This is not about letting our heart break for others because they are suffering, end of story. It's about letting our heart break for others and then *helping them out of their suffering.*

Sometimes new meditators get frustrated with the state of the world and want to go out and be angry with those they perceive as wrong and bad and yell in the streets. I've been there. When I was eighteen I was arrested and held for days because I thought the president was contemptible and his foreign-policy implementation was atrocious. I was so angry and did not hide my anger. I made sure anyone I perceived as having an opposing view from me felt it.

After that protest arrest, I realized that lashing out in anger wasn't serving anyone, least of all me. In fact, it was causing harm to myself and everyone I encountered. I began to take the meditation teachings more seriously, realizing that until I faced my anger 100 percent and saw the sadness underneath, I would not be able to benefit others.

Chögyam Trungpa Rinpoche once said, "If you put one hundred percent of your heart into facing yourself, then you connect with this unconditional goodness. Whereas if you only put fifty percent into the situation, you are trying to bargain with the situation and nothing very much will happen."[2]

When we sit our butts down on the cushion and commit to the practice, we are cultivating that 100 percent attitude of facing ourselves and our own suffering. This is the means by which we see our own way through to connect to our innate goodness.

From that place of goodness and enoughness, we can then look around and see that everyone else—those we like, dislike, or ignore—is also struggling. With this realization, we understand from our own lived experience that the number one thing we can offer these individuals is being there 100 percent with them.

We can still be activists, but we engage with others from a place of understanding and love. We can seek to be scientists and become curious about everyone we encounter, and through our new forms of understanding we offer them limitless love and aspire to be of benefit to them. This is compassion in action.

21 REJOICING IN JOY

Thich Nhat Hanh once wrote, "Life is filled with suffering, but it is also filled with many wonders, like the blue sky, the sunshine, the eyes of a baby. To suffer is not enough. We must also be in touch with the wonders of life."[1]

If you would do me a favor? After reading this paragraph, please put the book down for one minute. Take three deep breaths. Then look around you. Rest your mind. Take in the sights and sounds, the full range of perception. What can you appreciate about this moment? What wonders are present? Rest in that appreciation.

For me, I heard birds chirping outside. I sensed my daughter sleeping upstairs, peacefully curled up, warm and safe. I noticed plants I have cared for since before the pandemic that, despite the chaos in the world around them, continue to thrive. There are so many wonders if I slow down long enough to recognize them.

After exploring compassion, the capacity to bear witness to and aspire to alleviate the suffering of others, we can look at the Buddhist notion of *mudita*, or sympathetic joy. As Thich Nhat Hanh reminds us, there is indeed suffering. But Buddhism does not tell us to stop and wallow in the mire of that suffering. Instead, it encourages us to look to the present moment and liberate ourselves from it, connecting to our innate wakefulness and goodness as well as the joys that arise naturally.

When we are fully present, we can experience the many wonders of the world: the clouds rolling across the sky, the warmth of the sun on our skin, the company of loved ones. All of these simple moments are full of joy and bliss, yet we are often too lost in our own heads to discover them.

Similarly, because we spend so much of our time lost in the anxieties of the day, we rarely pause to celebrate others' joy. A playful dog or a laughing child might be reaching out to us, calling for our attention, yet we're buried in our devices, barely looking up. But when we do, we can pause and connect to whatever joy they emanate.

Earlier, I mentioned a pretty benign experience of driving behind a man enjoying a leisurely drive with his dog. Initially I had ignored them, then when I realized they were making me late I became annoyed. However, thanks to my meditation practice, I was able to pause and take pleasure in their joyride. A man and his dog, simply enjoying the journey. The pleasures of good company, of the warmth of the sun on one's face, of having the time and space to relax. I was able to experience happiness when witnessing their happiness. That, my friends, is mudita.

Imagine that you are at a coffee shop, waiting in line as usual. But instead of letting your mind drift into irritation or zoning out on your phone, you take a moment to observe the people around you. Perhaps you notice a barista who moves with skill and focus and genuinely seems to care about each customer. Or you overhear a conversation between friends, one of them laughing at her friend's jokes.

Instead of passing by these moments, you can pause to appreciate the joy and connection others are experiencing. This doesn't have to be a grand, profound moment—it's simply a shift in perspective, a reminder that joy is constantly flowing through the lives of others around us. By cultivating mudita, we open our hearts to these small, beautiful expressions of happiness in our everyday world.

There is tremendous joy we can experience when we rest in the present moment. This joy is magnified infinitely when we rejoice in the joy of others.

22 PRACTICES FOR CONNECTING WITH THE GOODNESS OF OTHERS

Over the course of this section, we have explored how to recognize basic goodness in other people—whether they are the people we like, the people we dislike, or even that vast group of people we don't put in either group and ultimately ignore.

One foundational practice we explored is learning to open up to the world around us with the eyes of understanding and love, recognizing everyone's humanity. This is why the mindfulness-awareness practice is key: it brings us in contact with our environment so that we enter the world and interact with others from a place of true presence. The bodhichitta and loving-kindness practices expand our capacity to go beyond focusing on ourselves and instead bear witness to the suffering and joy around us. The more connected we are to a larger awareness of the present moment, the more naturally understanding and love can grow.

In addition to these foundational practices, I'd like to offer a handful of on-the-spot exercises that are easy to integrate into your daily life and can deepen your connection to the basic goodness in others. Each practice is designed to gently broaden our compassion in everyday settings, helping us reframe the way we see and engage with others. Let's begin.

Deep Listening

The first exercise is deep listening, which is often easiest to practice with someone you might already place in the "people I like" group. When you're connecting with someone—during a phone conversation, a shared meal, or a catch-up with a friend—take the opportunity to practice deep listening.

This is not a complex practice, but it does take some focus. When this person is speaking, simply listen to them. That means resisting the urge to jump in with a story or interrupt with your own thoughts. It means setting aside judgment, even the subtle kind that arises when we're comparing things to our lived experience. It means not thinking through what you will say when it's your turn. Just be there with them. If you do, you'll find that this person feels more understood by you and you will be more skillful when it comes time for you to respond to them. These sorts of conversations often feel more meaningful to us. In these moments, both of you are given the space to relax into your basic goodness.

Pet Meditation

This next exercise involves another being in the "like" group: a pet. Yes, animals also possess basic goodness. I currently share my life with two basically good dogs and two basically good cats, all with their own personalities and quirks, which gives me plenty of opportunities to try this practice.

Whatever pet you have, take a portion of your day, perhaps morning or evening, and truly be present with them. Notice where they are in your home. When you are able, spend time with them intentionally. When you pet them, just pet them. When you walk them, just walk them. Resist the impulse to check your phone or think about your to-do list. Just be there with your loving animal as they headbutt or kiss you. You may find more joy in the eccentricities of your beast and your shared connection than in whatever's happening in your email inbox.

Loving-Kindness for a Friend

If you think you don't have time for a longer loving-kindness meditation, here is a short practice that can help you reconnect to bodhichitta on the go. I learned this exercise from the children's book *Mindful Tots: Loving-Kindness*, and it's wonderfully simple.

Bring to mind the image of a friend. Close your eyes and say their name silently. Rest your mind, relax, and let yourself hold the image of them gently. See if doing this stirs up warmth or tenderness. This quick exercise is a reminder that loving-kindness doesn't need to take long; even a moment's heartfelt attention can help you reconnect with bodhichitta.

Grocery Store Meditation

If you want to train in opening your heart to the "everyone else" group, the grocery store can be a surprisingly powerful setting for meditation. When you next go shopping, take it slow. Put your phone on airplane mode. Physically slow down your pace as you push the cart. Don't try to rush the experience. Aim to be present for what you are doing, but more important, try to be present with the people in the store with you. We often pass by others in the store without a second thought, but here, we're going to shift our view to make everyone we see a part of our experience.

The grocery store is full of people you likely do not know, who lead their own lives and have their own concerns. Try making eye contact. Smile. Say hello or give a nod. Engage them to the extent you are comfortable. Or you could even go a little bit beyond your comfort level and see what that feels like.

These days I have a baby with me when I go grocery shopping and she waves at everyone we pass. Sometimes they smile and wave back. Sometimes they ignore her (which breaks my heart a little). But overall, she inspires me to join in this practice with her, putting myself out there with a vulnerable and tender heart to engage in a moment of connection. The aim here is to not only be mindful but also to be kind. We are recognizing the basic goodness of everyone we encounter.

The Loving-Kindness Photo

Of everything I have asked of you, I imagine recognizing the basic goodness of someone you find difficult may be the hardest. Perhaps this practice will help you in opening your heart to them.

First, put a photo of this difficult person out in your home. I know, you don't want to. I realize it can be a bit triggering. I remember one meditation student saying, "Why in the world would I put my husband's ex-wife in our home? I don't even want to see her outside of it." You don't have to put the photo on your nightstand, it can be somewhere a bit more discreet—a bookcase maybe, or even in your wallet.

Whenever you see their photo, offer one of the loving-kindness aspirations: "May you feel happy" or "May you be safe," for example. Whatever aspiration for their well-being feels right and genuine to you, use that.

The more you train in opening your heart to this photo of your difficult person, the more open-hearted you will likely feel when you encounter them in person. The meditation student who was resistant to the photo of her husband's ex-wife? She now swears by this practice for helping her see past her initial feelings and more clearly recognizing this person's humanity and goodness.

Contemplating Understanding

Compared to our postmeditation practices for the other waking hours of our day, this practice can be added to your daily mindfulness meditation. See how I assume you are now practicing meditation daily?

After practicing mindfulness for a few minutes, ask the question, "Where has my understanding not yet reached?" Pause. Let your inner wisdom pipe up and answer for you. This is not an intellectual exercise where we try to figure anything out. Whatever answers come up from inside you are good. Just notice what comes up. After pausing for thirty seconds or so, ask the question again: "Where has my understanding not yet reached?"

Maybe you are generally a pretty understanding person, except for when it comes to that particular family member. Perhaps you have not spent much time trying to understand your work colleagues. Maybe you are understanding, except for members of that political party you detest. Whatever comes up, comes up. You might receive one answer several times or several different answers; both are fine.

"Where has my understanding not yet reached?"

After five minutes of this contemplation, close with a few more minutes of your mindfulness-of-the-breath practice. This willingness to explore where our heart shuts down and how much more we can open it leads us to living a more compassionate life based in understanding and goodness. With this simple question, you're gently inviting yourself to extend understanding a little further.

On-the-Spot Sympathetic Joy

Finally, we have a sympathetic-joy practice that you can do any time you're out and about. You could be in a park, wandering around a museum, or just strolling down the street. When you remember to do this practice, pause. Take three deep breaths, in through the nose and then out through the mouth. Feel the weight of your body through your feet.

When you feel a bit grounded, raise your gaze and look around you. You may feel an affinity for some people, an instant dislike for others, and the desire to actively ignore many more. Letting those judgments drop for now, just notice who is having a good time.

Your gaze may fall on a couple holding hands and laughing. Alternatively, you may see kids playing and running around like maniacs. Maybe there's someone just enjoying their own company, reading a book with a smile. Wherever you see joy, rest your attention there. Rejoice in their joy.

Then make an aspiration for their continued happiness. This could be "May your joy never diminish" or "May you continue to feel happy together." Whatever feels right to you, put that aspiration out there. In this way, you're connecting with the goodness of others and adding your own warmth and goodwill to the world.

These practices can help you deepen your connection to the basic goodness in others—whether it's in small, everyday encounters or in relationships where you've previously struggled to connect to bodhichitta. With time, these practices will lead you to a more compassionate, open-hearted way of relating to the world around you.

PART THREE

SOCIETY IS BASICALLY GOOD

23 SOCIETY ISN'T FUCKED UP

Having taken on the view of a scientist and gotten curious about ourselves, we find that we are more connected to our own basic goodness. This discovery may have inspired us to seek out the goodness in others, even those we find challenging or tend to ignore. Now we're ready to take another step: we move into the very big laboratory of exploring the basic goodness of society itself.

When we think of society, it often feels like an abstract force—something that happens out there. It's easy to conceptualize society as a vast, impersonal system that exists outside our immediate experience, shaping our lives without our direct influence. We might view it as a monolithic structure with rules, expectations, and power dynamics that we can't hope to change. Sometimes it feels like society acts on us, not the other way around.

We might conceptualize it as something we don't really connect to, that we rebel against or are subsumed by. We might think of ourselves as one insignificant speck of an overall larger whole or believe that we are unable to influence something as large as society.

That's a little grim, though, no? What if we approached society differently? Previously we talked about relating to the people we like, those that we don't like, and the ones that we normally ignore. Society is composed of eight billion people that we have sorted into those three groups. "Society" is a fancy term for all of us humans. In the same way a river is made up of many, many drops of water, society is made up of you and me and all those other beings. We are all part of an interconnected, shifting whole. Instead of viewing society as a distant, amorphous force, we can see it as a dynamic collection of individuals, each carrying their own basic goodness. As the Tibetan Buddhist teacher Traleg Rinpoche once said, "Societies . . . are not amorphous entities but are made up of a collection of individuals just like ourselves."[1] In other words, society isn't an entity separate from us—it's *us*.

Mini Societies: A New Perspective for Connection

Still feeling overwhelmed? Okay. Let's break it out into smaller parts.

Society isn't just an overwhelming sea of people; it's made up of countless mini societies, and you belong to many of them. Earlier, I said that we might think of society as something that happens out there, beyond the walls of our home. However, your home is a mini society unto itself. Currently, my home society is made up of me, my wife, a baby, two dogs, and two cats. When I first wrote this chapter I mentioned that we were expecting a baby girl and predicted that she would likely dominate the culture of our home society for some time. I was right.

Each of us plays a role in shaping our little home society. We have certain things we do and aim not to do. We like to spend our mornings in community together. Some of us go to work together (our older dog with my wife, our puppy with me). We discourage barking at strangers, as we don't deem it polite. And so on. There are certain values and ways we do things in my home society, which I imagine will look different from yours (perhaps you love barking at strangers over there).

Beyond the home, there are other societies we actively participate in. For me, there's my friend group, which is a group that bonds over shared interests rather than idle gossip. There's my CrossFit society, which is a local gym with a unique culture that encourages kindness and support for one another. There's the society of the meditation community I lead—The Basic Goodness Collective—which values, not surprisingly, basic goodness, understanding, and mindfulness for all. And then there's my Dad Fight Club, but we don't talk about Dad Fight Club (it's a group of dads who get together and forget to fight because we're too busy bonding over parenting tips).

Each of these mini societies has its own culture, yet they all contribute to the broader fabric of society. Also, the people in my friend group, gym, meditation community, and fight club have several of their own mini societies they take part in that also are a part of the larger society. You too likely have several societies you take part in that are part of the patchwork of society overall: your home society, your work society, your social group, and so on.

Here's the liberating truth: these societies didn't just form on their own; they were co-created by people, by *us*. These people have basic goodness, and so each one reflects the basic goodness of its members.

My home society is something I have actively co-created with the other beings that live with me. All of us have basic goodness and value that in our interactions. The same goes for my work society and friend groups; we connect through the lens of seeing one another's goodness.

Even when we join a preexisting society, like a gym, we remain active participants in shaping its culture. Our behavior can reinforce or challenge the prevailing norms, and we have a constant opportunity to infuse these spaces with kindness and understanding. For example, if I show up at the gym and start talking over the coach leading the class, being rude to other members and generally disrupting the flow of things, it is like pouring gasoline into a clear pool of water—the effects are immediately visible and radiate out. The other people may leave that day feeling hurt by me or upset that they couldn't concentrate on the class. Yet because so many of us do the polar opposite—showing up in a timely way, being respectful of one another, and exhibiting kindness—we naturally co-create a culture that is rooted in basic goodness, whether the owner of the gym would call it that or not.

This is how societies work: we all are active members co-creating positive or negative environments, based on whether we are in touch with our basic goodness or deeply disconnected from it. If several of us feel comfortable enough to be who we are, we are connected to basic goodness and often treat one another very kindly. If we feel threatened in some way, we are more likely to be suspicious of one another, undermine one another, and create more stress for the society overall.

This dynamic is true for every mini society. Whether it's a friend group, a workplace, or even a subway car, our actions influence the collective experience. Anyone who has spent any amount of time in New York City will know how lovely or horrific a subway mini society can be. You can get on the subway and luck out: people are generally quiet in your car and perhaps there's some kids sweetly playing with each other. People are smiling at them and one another. You feel safe and able to relax into this moment.

If you had gotten on the same train but two cars down, there might be some really drunk bros yelling over each other, absolutely not caring that they are ruining the experience of the people around them. Everyone is flinching, feeling subtly unsafe, trying to move away from them and feeling uncomfortable. Same train but a very different experience of a mini society, reflecting the power of individual actions within a shared space.

When you begin considering how you want to partake in all the various societies in your life, don't be a drunk bro on a train. Realize that your actions have ramifications on the society you are currently taking part in. You can be the respectful subway rider. You can be the kind person at the gym. You can be a loving member of your friend group. These individual roles can affect the overall dynamic of those mini societies in incredibly profound ways. Best of all, these mini societies are a part of and thus effect the whole of society overall.

Creating a Ripple Effect of Goodness

Our participation in these mini societies has a broader impact. Consider this: If you work in a grocery store, you may interact with hundreds of people in a single shift. Each time you engage with someone from a place of kindness and respect, you're acknowledging their basic goodness. That moment of connection could uplift their day, inspiring them to carry that goodness into their own interactions. This ripple effect can extend far beyond the walls of the store, subtly influencing countless other mini societies.

Even within larger, more formal institutions, the impact of basic goodness can be profound. I had the good fortune to teach meditation at the White House a few times. I remember a particularly large group being present for one session. I asked, "Who here has noticed someone from their department also attending meditation?" Almost everyone raised their hands.

When I asked a random person how many people were in her department, she told me there were a grand total of twenty. Also, that two of them were present that day for meditation. I am no mathematician, but that led me to believe that 10 percent of her department took time out of their busy day to prioritize mindfulness and meditation. Let's pretend for a moment that these two people began meditating regularly, such that these practices transformed their hearts and minds and allowed them to contact their basic goodness.

Now imagine those two people went to their twenty-person work society and began acting from that place of basic goodness. It would radically transform the relationships they had with everyone else in that office. Some of those people might get interested in meditation, others might not, but overall, basic goodness would begin to permeate the entire department when a simple 10 percent of the people there valued and exhibited it.

Multiply that effect times however many departments were represented that day and soon enough you have this major institution, the White House, operating from a place of basic goodness. That could be quite powerful. Many of our mini societies—work or otherwise—are similar in nature.

Society Is What We Make It

This is the magic of society. Society is not something we get swept up in and are subject to its whims. It's something we all are an active part of co-creating. It is an ever-evolving tapestry woven from the interactions of billions of mini societies. It's something we are constantly influencing with each interaction we have with one another. Every time we treat a stranger with kindness or seek to understand someone we initially perceive as difficult, we are touching in with our own basic goodness and inviting them to also recognize their own.

What is society? "Society" is a word we use to refer to all of us humans living on earth, each participating in our own mini societies. All people possess basic goodness. When we look at it from that perspective, society isn't fucked up. It's basically good. We can begin to look at all of the societies we take part in and realize that we in fact are the crucial element needed to move the needle within them from insensitivity or disregard to kindness, love, and joy.

We can be lanterns of basic goodness in each of our mini societies, shining on everyone we encounter, illuminating their basic goodness in kind. Even when things look rough for society, we always have a chance to touch in with our individual basic goodness and the basic goodness of everyone around us. This simple act helps us co-create a society that truly reflects our shared humanity—one that thrives on love, connection, and understanding.

24 YOUR LIFE IS YOUR LABORATORY

Sometimes people forget that the Buddha was a person—a guy named Siddhartha. The title *buddha* is actually a word they applied to him that can be translated as "awake" or "awakened one." Because our true nature is wakefulness, we are all buddha but have yet to truly realize it. Buddhism is less a dogma than a path of practice and individual understanding. It invites us to meditate in order to connect with our innate wakefulness and to study the teachings of the Buddha so that we can deepen that connection. In that way, you don't have to be a card-carrying Buddhist to practice Buddhism. We can *live* Buddhism by showing up for all of our many mini societies—work, home, friend group, and so on—from a place of embodied presence and connection with our basic goodness.

In the previous chapter, I used the term "laboratory" to describe our various mini societies. Each interaction within these mini societies presents an opportunity to experiment with mindfulness and basic goodness. For example, when I'm overwhelmed with work, my "work society" becomes an experiment in preoccupation. After my morning meditation, my mind begins thinking through my schedule and all the things that I need to do that day. When I am eating lunch I can get lost in thinking about my next meeting. At the end of the day, I check my calendar and think about what I have to do the next day. That is an experiment in preoccupation.

Alternatively, I can experiment with mindfulness in my work society. When I am in one meeting, I can simply be present for what that person is saying. When I am in the next, I am just completely present for them. When I eat lunch, I simply eat lunch. When I end my day, I end my day; I stop checking email and show up for the next society I am to take part in. Thus, I am experimenting with mindfulness and, as a result, with basic goodness in my work society. When I am done with my day, I am fully present with my family and engage in new experiments with my home society.

The Buddhist teacher Sharon Salzberg once said during a talk, "Mindfulness isn't difficult; we just have to remember to do it." When I mentioned that an experiment with mindfulness meant being 100 percent present with the people I was meeting with, I didn't say that I was actively *doing* anything. I wasn't working myself up to show up for them. I was simply there. This is an important distinction: trying to *do* Buddhism versus simply acting in an embodied way, connected to our basic goodness, which is *being* Buddhism. It is living Buddhism.

The more we practice meditation, the more there is a felt experience of basic goodness. That is important because when we begin to integrate the teachings of the Buddha, not just as a thing we're studying but as a way of living our life, it is the turning point in our spiritual path.

We have to make sure we do not separate our meditation practice—this thing we do for ten or twenty minutes every day—from the other waking hours of the day. There has to be a sense of integration if we are interested in living Buddhism. One definition of the word "integration" is "the act or instance of combining into an integral whole." This is the transition we can make from studying Buddhism and practicing meditation to living a life fully informed by the principle of basic goodness.

Rangjung Rigpe Dorje, the Sixteenth Karmapa, emphasized the point that every living situation can become a part of one's practice. We have the option to be living the practice instead of just doing it. This means that every living situation—brushing your teeth, being in conflict with your spouse, picking up the mail at the post office, catching up with family, driving, and so on—can become an opportunity to live your practice and embody basic goodness.

Allow me an example: I am not naturally a handy person. My wife and I bought a very old house some years ago and, as with many old houses, there is always something in need of fixing. Now I have bought some tools and I can watch YouTube videos, and some projects I can do and do well. But other projects? That's when we call in our handyman, Chris.

Unlike me, Chris has been fixing up old houses in our area for decades, and when he sees a problem, he is very methodical and easygoing about fixing it. I tend to try and find the right words to Google, then figure out how to do what the Internet tells me to do. Chris instinctively just does it. It's not an intellectual exercise for him. His experience has given him a calm confidence and the ability to see things for what they are and thus easily do what is needed.

Similarly, we don't need to intellectualize basic goodness. Chris didn't become skillful at his work because he spent decades watching YouTube videos about fixing old houses. He was initially guided on how to do some things while he got out there and experienced doing them, and eventually he grew to trust in himself to handle whatever arises. His experience is integrated into his being. Likewise, when it comes to basic goodness, once we've begun to experience it, we can trust in it and act from it naturally.

When it comes to our home society, if we end up in a conflict with our spouse, we shouldn't say, "What technique from that basic goodness book might work here?" We should trust ourselves by dropping into our own basic goodness, realizing the goodness of our partner and *being there* with them. That is integration. Our spouse can be pissed off at us, but we are here for it. We're embodied and confident in our basic goodness because we've been spending time experiencing it regularly. We *are* basic goodness in that moment.

"Yes, Lodro," you might be thinking, "but how do I approach all of my various mini societies / laboratories from a place of basic goodness?"

Well, honestly? Mindfulness meditation. I will not repeat the practices from previous chapters, but that is *the* way we come to not an intellectual but an experiential understanding of basic goodness. That said, I would like to offer some laboratories that you may want to experiment in to bring about the experience of basic goodness in your life.

Your Neighborhood

When you go for a walk in your neighborhood, try to inhabit your body. Feel your body move through space. Notice the tension in your legs. Pay attention as your shoulders begin to relax. This is about being in your body. Then, when you find yourself passing people on the street, acknowledge not just your basic goodness but theirs as well. This is bringing basic goodness into your neighborhood society and treating even a walk around the block as a laboratory.

Your Home

I find that in our home societies, we are often given opportunities to experiment with being present with basic goodness. Often I will be giving a Buddhist talk online and June, our puppy, will come in and start wandering around. Is she interested in whether she is disturbing me? No, she is interested in a bug. At some point she may come up to me and paw at me for attention. She is fully present, and when she comes to me, she is inviting me to experiment with being present with her. Instead of viewing this moment as an annoyance, I can accept the invitation to connect to basic goodness.

Your Family

Similarly, when we are around our family, they too are constantly inviting us to be in the moment with them. They pull on our sleeves and invite us to be here now, to show up and join them in the present. It's up to us to accept their invitation and experiment with being with things as they are or to continue to tend to other matters. When we drop what we consider to be so important, we open to the possibility of a shared understanding of basic goodness.

I once heard that Chögyam Trungpa Rinpoche said, "Taking the attitude that the phenomenal world is sacred is the first and last practice of all." When I talk about treating all of our mini societies as laboratories, this is how we do it. We take on the attitude of "Oh, I can experiment with basic goodness on all of these occasions. The world around me is sacred because it is inhabited by basically good beings. It is rife with invitations to be present. I can meet each invitation as it arises." It's not about labels or formalities, it's about cultivating a deep, lived connection to wakefulness in every situation.

Ultimately, this practice of integrating basic goodness transforms not only ourselves but also the world around us. Each act of mindfulness, each moment of kindness, ripples outward as a grand experiment, enriching our shared human experience. In this way, we're not just living Buddhism, we're co-creating a world rooted in basic goodness.

25 BASIC GOODNESS IN NATURE

Earlier I mentioned that taking the attitude that the phenomenal world is sacred is the most important practice of all. In my experience, nothing cultivates this attitude more effectively than time spent in nature.

I was born and raised in New York City and, to some extent, I'll always be a city kid. I would love to say that when my family moved to upstate New York in my preteen years I fell in love with nature, but frankly I resented leaving the big city. I would also love to say that in visiting my folks in my twenties I fell in love with nature. I didn't.

It's just in the last few years that my relationship with nature began to change. My wife and I moved out of New York City and into an old house that was built in the 1700s on Mohican land, across from an apple orchard. Here I've started to engage with the natural world in ways that feel simple yet transformative. I am able to pick my own fruits and vegetables across the street. I am able to walk barefoot in my yard and free the trees from invasive vines trying to hurt them. These simple acts of communing with nature have frankly changed me. They have opened my eyes to the basic goodness of the natural world.

Much of this book focuses on recognizing our own basic goodness and seeing it in others. But basic goodness isn't limited to human interactions. Nature is a profound teacher, offering endless invitations to connect with who we truly are. We can experience basic goodness simply by connecting to the natural world around us.

Right now, as I write, the tree outside my window is coming to life with delicate white flowers. All I have to do is shift my attention from the laptop to the tree limbs gently swaying in the wind to remember basic goodness, or notice the yellow tulips struggling to emerge and the birds chirping cheerfully, having recently returned from their long journey south. These simple, everyday phenomena are not just beautiful; they're gentle reminders of our interconnectedness and shared goodness.

Each morning, when I let the dogs run free in our yard, I take a moment to observe the trees. In the fall, the trees fully transform and many leaves will make their descent to the ground. I enjoy taking some time to watch their transition. Some leaves float, even dance, in their gradual journey from the tree to the earth. Others are clunkier, bashing against branches on their way down, almost like they are fighting this most natural of acts. There's a meditative quality to this observation, an opportunity to pause and witness the beauty in nature's cycles. These moments invite me to rest in basic goodness, to remember that I too am part of this sacred dance.

Chögyam Trungpa Rinpoche once said, "We experience glimpses of goodness all the time, but we often fail to acknowledge them. When we see a bright color, we are witnessing our own inherent goodness. When we hear a beautiful sound, we are hearing our own basic goodness."[1] Nature offers these glimpses constantly. We can experience basic goodness by bearing witness to the vibrant petals of a flower, the steady hum of the bees, or the warmth of the sun on our skin. All of these can be reminders of basic goodness, should we be present enough to acknowledge them.

I implore you to not be like me: don't wait for half your life to pass before fully opening to nature's wisdom. Let it support you in waking up to who you are. The trees in my yard have been around long before me and will be around for much longer than I will be here. They offer me lessons in patience and resilience. In its stillness and simplicity, the natural world mirrors back our own basic goodness. All we have to do is simply pause and let it speak to us.

26 DRALA

In Tibetan Buddhism, the term *drala* is often translated as "energy above aggression." This energy exists in our environment. It is most present when we're fully attuned to ourselves and the world around us. It is when we are fully connected to the wisdom of our own being and with the power of things as they are, where we are. To connect with drala, however, requires letting go of aggression—our clinging to irritation, resentment, or negativity.

Recently I attended a cocktail party for a group of artists who were displaying their work. The event was hosted by the painter John Morrow. One of his landscapes—a coastal scene of Majorca—caught my eye. I asked him something innocuous about it, and he said, "You know, that was one of the happiest days of my life."

He went on to share how the day began with frustration. He and a fellow artist had driven around for hours, searching for the perfect spot to paint. His friend was obsessed with finding a particular type of landscape. John kept recommending places, and every suggestion was rejected. Hours later, he grew very annoyed at his friend. Finally, they settled on the cove depicted in the painting. John told me, "At that point I had to make a choice. I could stay with my anger or I could let it go and appreciate the moment around me." He chose the latter and spent the day painting, enjoying time with his friends, eating delicious food, and relaxing. But, he was quick to point out, it only became one of his happiest days because he released his aggression and allowed himself to connect to the energy of the moment—what I would call drala.

In his book *The Relaxed Mind*, my root teacher Dza Kilung Rinpoche writes, "The Buddha spoke of how we can see one object in two different ways. When we are in a happy mood, with the mind more pure and open, whatever we see around us is inspiring and easy to connect with in a positive way. But if the day is not going so great, with difficult situations arising, even the flavor of the best meal in the best restaurant tastes flat. There's nothing wrong with the flavor of the food itself; it's the mind's negativity that makes everything different."[1]

In other words, the quality of our experience is shaped not by external conditions but by the state of our mind. We could be in the most beautiful cove with the most wonderful friends eating the most delicious food, and if we are clinging to our negativity we will enjoy none of it. To connect with drala—and thereby to basic goodness—we must let go of that inner aggression.

One mistake people make is that they think drala is just about being in nature. It's easy—maybe easier—to experience drala in nature. Nature often provides an immediate sense of awe and connection. Imagine walking down a wooded path that opens up to a stunning waterfall. In that moment there's a certain energy shift. You feel more open, more connected to your basic goodness, even more alive. There's something electric about that feeling.

But drala isn't exclusive to natural settings. Over a decade ago I got very annoyed at a Buddhist teacher. I was on a long retreat in the mountains of Colorado, sitting for long hours. This teacher introduced the principle of drala and gave example after example of experiencing the majesty of drala and uplifted energy . . . only when in nature. Then she said, "And you people from New York City? You can go to Central Park, I guess."

As a lifelong New Yorker, my hand immediately went up. "Are you saying drala can only be experienced in nature?"

She shrugged and nodded.

I then proceeded to list the number of occasions when I had a direct experience of drala in New York City, in resonance with the architecture and art, which I will share for any of you who are also city lovers and want to experience this phenomena yourselves:

- the moment you walk into the large atrium of a museum and your mind goes blank in response to the sheer profundity of it all
- gazing out of a high-rise window to notice the intricate gargoyle on a neighboring building that someone carved decades ago for no structural reason but because it uplifted the entire environment
- walking, biking, or driving across a bridge and viewing the powerful, energy-packed city skyline

I could go on and on, but I think you understand what I am referring to. Each of these moments holds the same electric quality as standing before a majestic waterfall. They are reminders that beauty and inspiration are always accessible when we relax into the present moment and open ourselves to the world around us.

Drala is the moment when we meet the elemental quality of reality as it is. It's all about meeting the world as it is, letting it show us the basic goodness inherent in ourselves and everything around us.

27 THERE IS A CLOUD FLOATING IN THIS SHEET OF PAPER

Earlier I briefly introduced the concept of emptiness. Now I'm going to attempt a deeper dive. Why? Because understanding emptiness is essential to grasping basic goodness. And while describing it is notoriously tricky—it's about as hard to describe as the space between two clouds—it's worth the effort.

There are two forms of emptiness worth discussing in this context: the emptiness of self and the emptiness of other. Let's start with the emptiness of self. I touched on this in an earlier chapter when discussing compassion. Emptiness of self involves letting go of our fixed views, misconceptions, and biases so we can meet reality more genuinely as it is. It is also the realization that we are not a single, unchanging entity. All of the labels we put on ourselves, both good and bad, need to be dropped in order for us to meet our true face. That is the essence of no-self. As Thich Nhat Hanh once wrote, "There is a simple and general way to explain no-self, which is that there is no single entity whose identity is changeless."[1] We are in constant flux, shaped by countless conditions.

Next, there is the emptiness of other. This is where we begin to realize that everyone and everything around us similarly lacks an everlasting, fixed, permanent version of what they are. The world is dynamic, always shifting. The seasons are good reminders for us. When I look outside in April, I see new leaves blooming on our trees where a month before there was nothing. Months from now those leaves will fall to the ground. This cycle has been going on since before I was born and will continue long after I am dead. This thing I call a backyard is never the same from one moment to the next.

The same is true for everything around us. Thich Nhat Hanh has said, "If you are a poet, you will see clearly that there is a cloud floating in this sheet of paper. Without a cloud, there will be no rain; without rain, the trees cannot grow; and without trees, we cannot make paper. The cloud is essential for the paper to exist. If the cloud is not here, the sheet of paper cannot be here either. So we can say that the cloud and the paper inter-are."[2] This term "inter-are" points to the truth of interdependence. It is not just that things are empty of everlasting form and so nothing matters and life is meaningless. That would be nihilism, not Buddhism.

In the earliest teachings of the Buddha, it famously says, "Form is emptiness. Emptiness also is form." In other words, every form around us—the trees, this book, our families—lacks this nature of being just the one thing that we normally conceive of it as being. Rather, conglomerations of parts come together to present in a form we then name "tree," "book," or "family."

And yet, emptiness arises as form. You are able to hold this book and (I hope) get something useful out of it. So it's not *just* empty. The clouds and rain and trees come together to make up the paper of this book and this book is something that you can read. As His Holiness the Seventeenth Gyalwang Karmapa, Ogyen Trinley Dorje, once said, "When you first hear the term 'emptiness,' you might think this suggests nothingness or a void, but actually 'emptiness' here should remind us that nothing exists in a vacuum."[3] In other words, emptiness isn't a negation of existence but a reminder that everything is interconnected. Life unfolds in a web of relationships, and it is through this interdependence that we begin to see the profound truth of basic goodness.

Let's make this idea more tangible: I affect you and you affect me. I've spent a good amount of time putting these words on paper, hoping they'll help you realize your basic goodness. When you reach out to tell me, "This book helped me," I smile and it reminds me that this work matters. Simply by engaging with these words, you and I are connected.

This connection isn't limited to writer and reader. Whatever we do and wherever we are, we have an effect on those around us. When we realize the nature of emptiness, we see that we're constantly shaping and being shaped by the ever-changing world around us. When you wave someone ahead of you in traffic, you are acknowledging the truth of interdependence. You recognize that you're not the only one on the road and that your safety depends on the cooperation of others. You are offering compassion to your fellow driver in putting their needs before your own.

It might not seem like much, but this interaction is part of a larger, unseen network—a society of commuters, all working together to navigate the same roads. Anyone who has the same commute everyday will tell you that lots of people come together to form the "getting-to-work society." The way we show up, even from the relative privacy of our own car, will affect everyone around us and thus influence that society.

This principle applies to every aspect of our lives. The more we meditate, the more clearly we see things for the way they truly are, including the environment around us and the various societies we take part in. We begin to let go of our own habitual, not-so-helpful ways of thinking and doing. We start to recognize the fluidity of our own identity as well as the fluidity of everything around us. What once seemed fixed is actually dynamic and interdependent.

Here's the key takeaway from contemplating interdependence: you are always influencing the world around you. Whether you realize it or not, your actions ripple out, shaping the societies you're part of. The real question is: *Do you want to engage with the world from a place of confusion or from a place of basic goodness?*

28 BASIC GOODNESS IN THE NEWS

If I were you at this point, I'd be done with the Pollyanna basic goodness stuff. Basic goodness in the subway car, and being in nature, and drala at the museum is nice, but what about that moment when you open your favorite news site and immediately feel bombarded by negativity? Society doesn't always *feel* basically good.

Not to date myself, but back before the internet there was a time when we would get our news in one dose through a morning newspaper, process it, and then move on with our day. Now it feels like every major news outlet prides itself on breaking as many stories as quickly as possible, filling in clarifying details about them as they trickle in. This has led to a nonstop news cycle that stresses everyone out (including the people who work for these networks).

An analogy comes to mind: the ocean. I like the ocean a lot. I like standing in the water up to my knees. Looking out at the horizon, seeing the true depth of the ocean, can feel quite peaceful. However, if I wade in a little further beyond my comfort level and lose my ability to touch the ground or tread water, then it starts to feel a bit overwhelming. I start getting battered around by the waves and lose track of which way is which. I might get scared, feeling like I may never see land again.

The same dynamic can be applied to our relationship with the news. With healthy boundaries, we can engage with the news in a meaningful, manageable way. But if we go further than what our boundaries allow, frantically hitting refresh on our news story of choice over and over again, we risk being swept away. We then lose perspective and feel as though the world is perpetually on the brink of collapse.

Here's the key with both examples: *you* get to decide whether you stay on the metaphorical shore or plunge into the deep. You control whether you process the news in a way that feels manageable or overwhelm yourself by constantly exposing yourself to it.

Much of who we are comes down to the choices we make. We can choose to dwell on disturbing news, unresolved work conflicts, or issues with our family, or we can decide to channel our mental energy in more constructive ways, resting in the present moment and in connection to basic goodness. We know that basic goodness only exists in the here and now. It's not something you'll find when spiraling into "What if?" scenarios about the past or future.

Earlier, I mentioned boundaries. For me, that often looks like I read my news aggregate over coffee in the morning, pausing after each story to let it sink in. Then I re-enter my day informed but not drained by the experience. If there's breaking news, I'll set aside time to engage with it, process it, and then return to what I was doing before, but that isn't a daily occurrence. This is what works for me. You will likely have a different version for boundaries around news consumption that works for you.

The important thing is to reflect on what's serving you and what's not. This goes beyond the news—whether it's your work routine, social-media habits, or family dynamics, tuning in to what uplifts versus what drains you is crucial. Once you discern those patterns, you can employ the discipline to follow through on setting and maintaining boundaries that protect your peace and align you with basic goodness.

The Parrot and the Forest Fire

Relatedly, there is an old story from the Jataka tales about a brave parrot. One day, the forest where the parrot lived caught fire. The flames spread rapidly, endangering all the creatures who called the forest home. Now a parrot has wings, so the bird's first instinct was to fly up and away to safety. But as she ascended, she heard the cries of her fellow forest-dwellers. Overcome with compassion, she decided to act. She swooped into a nearby river, soaking her feathers in water, then flew back to the fire, shaking off the droplets over the flames. Back and forth she went, tirelessly trying to extinguish the fire, ultimately getting burned herself as she struggled to save everyone.

Meanwhile, in what is referred to as the god realm, divine beings were watching this parrot. They laughed at the sight of this tiny bird's futile efforts. Their mockery caught the attention of Indra, the king of the gods, who was curious to see for himself. Transforming into a mighty eagle, he flew down to meet the parrot.

"What are you doing?" Indra asked. "You're not really making much of a difference and you're about to be burned alive. Get out of here!"

The parrot, undeterred, replied, "You're a much bigger bird than I am. I don't need your advice. I need your help."

Indra was so moved by the courage and conviction of this small bird that he began to cry. His divine tears, far more powerful than the parrot's waterdrops, poured down, extinguishing the flames and saving the forest. Some tears fell on the parrot herself, healing the burned feathers and making them grow back in colorful hues. Thus the parrot's courage and compassion not only saved the forest but she became more beautiful than ever.

I was so moved when I heard this tale. Like the parrot, many of us feel compassion when faced with the world's suffering, especially as presented in the news. Yet we're often paralyzed by the belief that our small actions can't make a real difference. We tell ourselves, "I'm just one person. How can I help refugees overseas? How can I make a dent in systemic injustice from my small corner of the world?" So what do we tend to do? We curl up and feel broken-hearted. I get that. I get the proclivity to open your heart wide and then feel burned by the inability to do something tangible to help others.

Yet this parrot said, "No. I am going to overcome my hesitation and fear and try to do something to help, even if I end up hurt as a result." May it be that more of us develop that type of conviction, to try and help even at the risk of hurting ourselves. Furthermore, the parrot didn't just save her friends. She vowed to help all the animals in the forest, which I imagine included those she didn't like and didn't know. Her compassion was vast enough to include them all.

I think if the parrot had persevered and had somehow been able to put out the fire herself, this tale wouldn't have much teeth to it. But the crucial point is that the parrot didn't put out the fire alone. Her efforts drew attention to the crisis, inspiring Indra to step in and amplify her work.

In today's terms, that's the rough equivalent of tweeting something important and having it get retweeted by a celebrity with a very big platform. These days we have a lot of means of getting the word out about how we are trying to help. It's unpopular to go around saying, "This is my way of being of service" on Instagram or TikTok, but I think the platforms would be much healthier places to spend our time if that were the case. We live in a time where small acts of service, when shared, can ripple out in unexpected ways.

I am guilty of this too, by the way. Though my time is limited these days owing to caring for a baby, I still lead a donation-based meditation class every week, with all proceeds going to local nonprofits. It feels like my version of carrying waterdrops to a fire. But it's my contribution, my tiny offering to a world on fire, and I hope it will raise awareness that we can all do small things that can help. Yet how often do I share about my work to uplift the cause? Not enough, in my self-estimation. I'm reminded that shining a light on our contributions—no matter how small—can encourage others to join in and expand the impact.

Returning to our story, Indra's response to the parrot's plea is a profound lesson. He asks what she's doing and offers sound advice to get away and save herself. Instead of taking it and caving in to the urging of the bigger bird, the parrot invites him to get involved: "I don't need your advice. I need your help."

This one hit me. We live in a world filled with opinions and advice, self-proclaimed experts, and new fads. I don't know about you, but when things are going wrong in the world or I myself am struggling I don't need people to weigh in online and offer their hot take. I need them to roll up their sleeves and find their own way of helping.

Indra was so moved by this request that he did what was asked of him: he helped. Indra's tears didn't just put out the fire, they left the parrot in even better shape than before. This demonstrates that when we ask for help and receive it, we not only address the immediate problem but also grow stronger and more resilient in the process.

And here's the twist. That brave parrot? In the Buddhist tradition, she is said to be a past life of the Buddha himself. We possess the same seed of awakening as the Buddha, and his example teaches us that we can follow in his footsteps with similarly tremendous results.

In short, when we are faced with the seemingly insurmountable, all we can do is show up authentically and fully as ourselves, just as the parrot did. We may not be able to solve every issue we face alone, but thankfully we don't have to. We can raise awareness and let our example serve as a beacon to others, inviting them to get involved as well. Together, we can create powerful, collective change. And in the process we too may find ourselves transformed in ways we never imagined.

Vedana in the News

There's a wonderful series of talks by the Buddhist teacher Dr. Larry Ward titled *Beyond the News*.[1] In them he points to our habitual way of engaging with the news: we break stories up into the ones we like, the ones we don't like, and, you guessed it, the ones we actively ignore.

Whatever boundaries you put in place, I recommend engaging in what is known as the mindfulness of *vedana* (pleasant, unpleasant, and neutral feeling tones) when you read news stories. This is simply noticing that when you read a story that supports how you think, you tend to like it. When you read about a horrific injustice, you do not like it. That leaves many stories that we tend to gloss over and ignore.

When we encounter news that aligns with our views, it often inflates our sense of ego. In a Buddhist sense, ego refers to the stories we construct about ourselves—our identity, values, and affiliations. Reading a story about "people like us" doing good can bolster this narrative. We say, "Yeah! People like me are doing good things," and we let it reinforce, for example, the stories we tell ourselves about what a good liberal or conservative we are. As minor as that moment may be, it is one of many ways that we separate ourselves from the world around us. We draw lines in the sand of "me and my people" versus "those people over there," and that actually leads to us cutting others out of our open, awake heart and shutting down our connection to basic goodness.

Conversely, when you read a story that you don't like, it's not uncommon to feel aversion and to condemn people we have never met before. We mentally label these people as adversaries, shutting them out of our hearts. In both cases, we're reinforcing division and limiting our capacity for compassion.

That brings us to the fact that most people we read about in the news are strangers that we have never met. It is amazing to me how quickly we tend to shift from "I don't know this person" to "Do I like this person or dislike this person?" Our ego makes us ask that question from the point of view of are they for me and my agenda or against me and my agenda? The news is largely made up of people that we don't know, and this habit prevents us from seeing people as they truly are—complex beings, just like us, striving in their own ways.

Practicing the mindfulness of vedana can help us break this cycle. As you read the news, notice how you divide individuals into the people I like, the people I dislike, and everyone else. Pause and reflect: every person in those stories, whether you like, dislike, or ignore them, possesses basic goodness. They are, like you, doing their best within their circumstances and ability to connect to their basic goodness. We can see all the beings in the forest as a whole and have compassion for all of them.

Recall that every person you read about possesses basic goodness. Every single one. This gives us a perspective that is more equanimous. Like the parrot flying over the forest or a calm observer standing at the ocean's edge, we can remain steady, connected, and open-hearted, no matter what the news brings.

29 BOUNDLESS LOVE

Equanimity is often a desired result of meditation. Many people think that the term "equanimity" denotes feelings of peace and calm. In Buddhism, however, equanimity carries a deeper meaning. The Sanskrit term *upeksha* is commonly translated as "equanimity," but it can also mean "impartiality" or "inclusiveness." It is the fourth of the four types of limitless love, or the four immeasurables, introduced in chapter 9, alongside loving-kindness, compassion, and sympathetic joy.

Equanimity is the notion that when we loosen our fixed ideas about who we can offer our heart to, we make it wide enough to include absolutely everyone. We realize that we don't have to be partial with our love. It can be inclusive of all beings, everyone in society. It's not just about finding inner peace, it's about cultivating a profound and boundless love. Thich Nhat Hanh captured this beautifully when he said, "Make your heart large so that you may be able to see that the conditions for your happiness are there, and injustice, cruelty, or meanness is not enough to ruin your life. You can accept it easily, because your heart is large, and you can receive it without resentment and anger."[1]

This reframes love not as a limited resource but as something inherently abundant. Instead of coming at the idea of love from the perspective of a poverty mentality—What about me? What if I don't have enough to offer to others?—we realize that our love is boundless. It can hold everything and everyone we encounter, no matter how challenging or painful.

This means we can keep our heart open in all situations: when we read the news, when we are in the same subway car as drunk bros, when our partner is mad at us, all of it. Whenever we bear witness to injustice, cruelty, or meanness, we don't let it destroy our capacity to love. We receive it in our hearts, daring to look at the perpetrators through the lens of basic goodness, not letting resentment or even anger cloud our ability to offer them love.

It makes no sense to break the world up into people you like, people you don't like, and people you really couldn't care less about. They are all people. You are a person. We are all interconnected. In fact, we are all a society. We offer our love to us, and "us" includes everyone.

Thich Nhat Hanh illustrated this form of love with a powerful metaphor. Imagine throwing dirt into a glass of water. That water would be undrinkable, right? But throw that same clod of dirt into a river, and it will not destroy the river. The river remains vast, powerful enough to accommodate the dirt and transform it overnight into mud. People can still drink from the river because its capacity is so immense. Thich Nhat Hanh concluded by saying, "So practice being like a river, that is what the Buddha recommended to us."[2]

As we begin to see that basic goodness exists not only in ourselves but in all beings, we open our hearts wider. We must realize that we can offer our heart to everyone. There is not one person out there not worthy of our love and understanding. The only requirement is our willingness to make space for all beings.

30 BASIC GOODNESS IS BIGGER THAN SOCIETY

Previously, I mentioned the art tour and celebration of local artists held by my small town of a few thousand people. Yet within that incredibly small population, three hundred people signed up to participate in exploring art that weekend. When I heard that I felt so inspired. "Wow," I thought, "I live in such a cultured, sophisticated place!"

Then my friend Rich, who was in his drag persona Trixie Starr at the time, broke some disheartening news. Our local library had received a phone call: one town member had complained at length about them hosting a drag-queen story hour during the Pride celebration that month. One person in our small town felt compelled to speak out against an event meant to foster joy and inclusivity.

Later that evening, my wife and I went out for Mexican food and were debriefing about our night. I noticed the incredible joy I experienced when I learned how many people were supporting the arts that weekend. I then noticed the incredible sadness I experienced when I learned that someone had called to complain about our local drag queen's story hour. My wife, wise as ever, pointed out an obvious truth: there were three hundred people I was happy about and one that upset me. Yet the one complainer seemed to command the same amount of my mental attention. Having realized that, I was able to let go and move on.

This realization got me thinking. How often do we let one or two voices of discontent overshadow the goodness around us? When we consider that society is made up of a lot of (what we perceive as not great) people, we might get disheartened and ignore some of the good around us. Maybe you're like me and have a tendency to focus on the one jerk in a crowd of several hundred people. Take it from me: it's not a great way to spend your mental energy.

Furthermore, we can acknowledge that the one jerk, or all of the confused people we can imagine, possess basic goodness . . . but how many of *them* realize it? Are they even trying to be less of a jerk day in and day out? How many are actively trying to reduce their own confusion and be kinder, more compassionate people? Why can't they just realize they are innately peaceful and good already? It's tempting to dwell on these questions, to wish that others would recognize their intrinsic peacefulness and goodness. But, again, that's not a productive use of our mental energy.

Disheartenment is a real thing: we might feel it when we read the news, hear gossip about people we know, or see people litter in the street. Basic goodness can feel absent in society at those times, but that is partly because we are focusing on the wrong things. In contemplating this topic I remembered what my teachers always remind me: basic goodness can accommodate everything and everyone. Dza Kilung Rinpoche once wrote, "What we need most is trust—trust in the mind's ability to cultivate this really deep connection. The purity we are seeking is not in the nature of 'pure' versus 'impure.' If those opposites arise in our minds, we relax with them both rather than hoping for and trying to grab the 'pure,' and fearing and trying to push away the 'impure.' We relax and let that duality, that labeling, calm down."[1]

Here Rinpoche reminds us to trust in the mind's ability to connect to our innate wakefulness, our buddha nature. This is often referred to as a sense of purity, but he points out that it transcends the dualistic language of "pure" and "impure." It's only when we drop our dualistic notions that we truly relax into our inherent state, our basic goodness. As humans, we have a strong tendency to cling to what we perceive as good and pure and push away what we perceive as bad or impure. But it's the labeling itself that becomes a problem.

Relatedly, it's easy to ignore that there are some people doing good out there and instead focus on a bunch of other people who are basically acting like shitheads. But when we begin to relax that duality, that labeling, we can begin to see things more clearly. There's no need to split the world into "good people" and "bad people." We're all human and we all possess basic goodness.

When we talk about basic goodness, it is not the opposite of people possessing basic badness; it exists beyond such dualities. It is vast enough and intrinsic enough to who we are that it can accommodate and swallow our puny dualistic notions of "good" and "bad." Basic goodness is a wholeness, an enoughness that is beyond those labels.

Perhaps an example will help clarify my point. The sky is vast and spacious, like our basic goodness. The sky is not partial about the clouds that move through it. It does not like fluffy white clouds and dislike gray storm clouds. It holds space for all of them, impartial and vast. Similarly, our basic goodness accommodates everything: our purest intentions and best deeds, as well as our missteps and the mistakes we make. Basic goodness does not discriminate. It is not a reward system where we get good goodness points for helping an elderly lady across the street and can cash them in later for rewards, like at a Chuck E. Cheese.

When you do something kind, it is good good—good acts arising amid the background of basic goodness. When you do something harmful, it is bad good—bad acts arising amid the background of basic goodness. Our basic goodness does not vanish when we act from a place of confusion. It doesn't take a night off. It is still there, acting as a backdrop even as we ignore it and choose to act from our confusion and pain.

The same can be said for everyone else in society. Instead of getting lost in the news story, the gossip, or the litterer, we can look beyond any given moment of confusion to try to see basic goodness more clearly. We can expand our view to look at the background of society instead of focusing on the one jerk obstructing our view.

Yes, a lot of people out there act out of confusion. That does not negate their individual basic goodness or the goodness of society overall. It just means we need to look beyond the surface level of things and see clearly past the clouds to recognize the sky itself. We need to train our minds and hearts to not get lost in the pettiness of whatever turmoil is happening in this moment—our own or in the world around us—and lose track of what matters.

Basic goodness matters. It is, in my personal opinion, the thing that matters the most. Remembering our own basic goodness and the basic goodness of those around us puts us in touch with their humanity and keeps us from getting disheartened when we see jerks out there.

Chögyam Trungpa Rinpoche once said it well: "It is not just an arbitrary idea that the world is good, but it is good because we can *experience* its goodness. We can experience our world as healthy and straightforward, direct and real."[2]

Basic goodness is something we can perceive if we stop focusing so much on the surface-level turmoil and see the situation more fully for what it is. When contemplating the nature of society, don't just stare at the clouds. Look at the sky.

31 LIVING A LIFE WITHOUT REGRET

The Australian author Bronnie Ware compiled a poignant list in her book *The Top Five Regrets of the Dying*, based on her years of experience as a nurse. These five regrets reveal deep truths about how people often wish they had lived their lives differently:

1. I wish I'd had the courage to live a life true to myself, not the life others expected of me.
2. I wish I hadn't worked so hard.
3. I wish I'd had the courage to express my feelings.
4. I wish I had stayed in touch with my friends.
5. I wish that I had let myself be happier.[1]

Let's break these out one by one.

1. I wish I'd had the courage to live a life true to myself, not the life others expected of me.

One of life's greatest challenges is showing up authentically. To live meaningfully, we must align with our most genuine selves, which means being in touch with our basic goodness. A life spent conforming to others' expectations is a life misspent.

A lifetime is made up of years, which is made up of days, which is made up of hours, which is made up of minutes. To lose hours and days to anxiety and worrying what others may think of you is a life that will be wasted. Period.

2. I wish I hadn't worked so hard.

I get that some of us (myself included) take great joy in our work, while others live for the weekend, so to speak. Yet even those of us who enjoy work shouldn't work to the point that it dominates our lives. I have had times where the excitement around a new business venture pushes me to the extent that I lose sleep and eat poorly, neglecting to take good care of my body. "It's just this stage of getting the business running," I'd say to myself. But here's the thing: work will always have another stage, another task, another goal.

We've all heard the story of the corporate executive who suffers a breakdown, escapes to Bali, and returns as a yoga teacher or spiritual guide. It's weird how often I hear that story these days. It's actually a reflection of a broader societal issue: our glorification of overwork. Way too many of us push ourselves past the point of exhaustion to a breaking point. The lesson here isn't to reject work but to set boundaries.

Whenever I found myself running around and working too hard, I'd reflect on these tales and calm the f- out, taking a day off or sleeping in or exercising so I could course correct and remember life outside of work. These days, even with a kid, I find a pretty good balance between work I enjoy and enjoyment of life outside of work.

There will always be more to do. But life exists outside of deadlines and email inboxes. We need to find balance by prioritizing presence and joy, not just productivity.

3. I wish I'd had the courage to express my feelings.

Earlier, we discussed mindfulness of emotions as a means to connect with not just how we feel but how, instead of fighting against our feelings, we can allow them to move through us. When we practice mindfulness of emotions, we are less reactive and less likely to lash out, more able to see what we are feeling, and more skillful in communicating our emotions to others.

I was the first person in my friend group to lose a parent. I vowed, based on my experience, to help my friends through the experience when their time came. I've seen many of my loved ones and the loved ones of my loved ones die along the way. This is part of living a human life rich with connection. However, one thing I have always found comfort in is that my loved ones, when it's their turn to go, always know how much I love them. I am not shy in telling them that. I'd like to think that my doing so has inspired my friends to do that more as well. We never know how long any of us have. Life is too short to leave love unspoken. It is important to tell people how much they mean to you. It's important to say "I love you."

4. I wish I had stayed in touch with my friends.

In his earliest teachings the Buddha talked about the importance of having a community and spiritual friends, beings who support you in becoming the best version of yourself and who encourage you to live from a place of basic goodness.

One of my closest friends died in 2012, and it's a wound that will never entirely heal for me. Even writing this feels like scratching it open anew. Losing him taught me the importance of nurturing friendships and cherishing the time we have with them. As a result, I continuously work to stay in touch with my friends and let them know just how much they mean to me.

I hope you don't have to go through what I did in order to overcome this potential regret. I also hope that you are able to connect to your own community of like-minded, supportive individuals who can reflect your basic goodness back to you. Along those lines, you are warmly invited to the meditation community I lead—The Basic Goodness Collective—if you're looking for these kinds of spiritual friends (lodrorinzler.com).

5. I wish that I had let myself be happier.

What makes us feel happy? It's not lining up the most relaxing day with the perfect people. It's letting go of anything that holds us back from the present moment. I once heard Thich Nhat Hanh express that all we need to do to avoid regret is take care of the present moment.

I love that. All we have to do to avoid these many forms of regret is enter the present moment fully, remaining embodied in our basic goodness. There is no one who can let you be happy but you. Only you have the power over your own mind and the ability to make choices that lead you to suffering or to joy.

The Six Paramitas: Transcendental Actions for a Life Without Regret

The distinction between suffering and joy can be found in living a life of regret or living a life that is of benefit to ourselves and others. As we reflect on these five regrets, we see how easily our lives can slip into patterns of missed opportunities and unfulfilled potential.

But Buddhism offers us an antidote in the form of the six paramitas: generosity, discipline, patience, diligence, meditative concentration, and prajna. These transcendental actions guide us toward living with greater clarity, intention, and compassion, helping us to avoid the regrets we might otherwise carry. Each paramita offers a skillful way to engage with life fully, transforming moments of potential regret into opportunities for growth and connection.

Generosity

Generosity is the ability to let go of everything we normally cling to in the hope of propping up ourselves and our agendas. When we experience the wisdom of this very moment, we naturally begin to see opportunities for generosity. We can offer material things, such as money, a couch for someone to sleep on, letting a friend borrow our car, and more. We can also offer our time, a shoulder to cry on, or sage advice based in our lived experience. When someone is feeling threatened, we can stand up for them, generously offering our presence to protect them from fear or harm. There are many ways to be generous if we are attuned to the present moment.

Discipline

Discipline here is a sense of not escaping or running away from the present moment. We are willing to be here, truly present, for the good, bad, and ugly of our lives. This means we apply discipline to befriending the mind, leaning into our formal meditation practice so that we can live our lives in a more present manner. This also means we are present enough to know when someone could use our help, and we apply discipline to overcome any hesitation we may feel to show up for them and do whatever is required of us. We should remain vigilant about ways to help the world around us.

Patience

Patience invites us to take the long view. I once congratulated a politician friend for getting a bill passed. He smiled and said, "Funny thing is, I probably won't be around to see the benefits of this law." He understood that the greatest impact might come decades later, yet he still gave his all. This is a powerful reminder of patience as a long-term perspective.

Most of the time, though, when we talk about patience we think of someone pushing our buttons. A toddler asking "Why?" for the millionth time or someone in line ahead of us taking way too long to order. Even when someone wrongs us, even slightly, we can choose not to perpetuate anger, instead cultivating tolerance and compassion.

There is a Chinese proverb that says, "Slander cannot destroy an honest man . . . when the flood recedes the rock is there." I've found this to be true. Whether someone has said something unkind or outright false about me, taking the long view has always brought clarity. Traditional Buddhist texts even say that we should happily take on discomfort and suffering, because this is how we grow as spiritual people. It's not the medicine we want to take; it is, however, the medicine that heals us.

Another form of patience in Buddhism involves aspiring to a true understanding of reality. This means trying to adopt a broader perspective than we would normally take, examining the complexity of any given situation and determining the most skillful way to respond. In my experience, this sometimes looks like giving a lot of space and time to a complex issue, which leads to a more effective, long-term solution.

Diligence

Sometimes called "joyous effort," diligence is the idea that when we are fully present we are more able to leap in and help those around us. We notice the person struggling with their groceries or the stressed mother who just dropped their child's toy. Because we are present, we not only see the situation but we act to be of help to them, often without consciously thinking of it.

It's said we could wear our diligence like armor, never taking a break from it. Armed with this vigilance in seeking out opportunities to be of benefit to others, we find ourselves more willing to drop our habitual patterns and distractions and act in ways that help ourselves and others. It feels good to help. We then want to do more of it.

Similarly, we can apply this joyous exertion to our meditation practice. We can always think about how to go further in understanding ourselves so that we reduce the unintentional harm we cause in the world. Through diligence, we contribute to making the world a better place.

Meditative Concentration

The fifth activity appears to be one you've been doing all along: meditating. Yet here, meditative concentration implies a post-meditation aspect as well. We learn to develop a concentration that allows for a feeling of well-being, meaning we more readily give up distractions and are willing to live a simpler life without always craving for more, more, more.

These practices also lead to us embodying excellent qualities: we become kinder, gentler, and just overall more authentically ourselves. The more we are fully present with ourselves, the more we are able to bring our true presence to everyone around us.

Prajna

When we take enough care to enter the present moment, we see things as they are. This is known as *prajna.* To break that out from the Sanskrit, *pra* can be translated as "super" or "superior," and *jna* as "knowing" or "knowledge." It is considered superior to regular knowledge because it is the ability to look at, be present to, and understand reality as it is. Thus it is sometimes simply translated as "wisdom." It is what makes all of these other activities transcendent.

This is why the six paramitas are sometimes translated as "transcendental actions," or "perfections." I think we in the West are always striving to be some perfect (read: other, better) version of ourselves and thus miss the point of these practices, which is to reveal that we are already whole, complete, and good as is. So I tend to avoid using the word "perfections" in public talks so as to avoid inadvertently leading people into wishing they could become some perfect version of themselves.

The term "transcendental actions" might feel clunkier, but it captures the essence of these practices: they help us move beyond focusing just on ourselves and open our hearts to the world. A life based in service to others is a life worth living. By embodying these qualities, we can live a life free of regret.

32 ENLIGHTENED SOCIETY IS RIGHT NOW

Over the course of this book we have explored what are known as the three *yanas* or vehicles of Buddhism. There is the foundational vehicle, which is about the work we do to liberate ourselves from the trap of doubt and delusional thinking so as to wake up to our basic goodness. Then there are the Mahayana teachings, such as cultivating bodhichitta, practicing the four immeasurables, and engaging in the six paramitas, to connect more open-heartedly with everyone around us. Finally, we arrive at the Vajrayana teachings, known as tantric Buddhism.

In popular culture, the word "tantra" is often misunderstood, carrying connotations of sex and ecstatic bliss. But tantric Buddhism is far from the romanticized image mainstream society presents. So what is the grand secret of the Vajrayana? I'll tell you: *You are already enlightened. You just need to discover your basic goodness, develop a relationship with it, and live your life through its lens.*

Wait a minute. Isn't that where we started with this book? Yes. Yes, it is. The entire Buddhist path, including the very secret, very sexy tantric teachings, is about recognizing the potential to connect to your buddha nature in every minute of every day.

If we look at the Tibetan word for tantra, *gyu,* we see that it literally means "continuity." But continuity of what? It is the continuity of experiencing our own basic goodness. You wake up in the morning and, for a moment, feel into your body, perhaps sense the warmth of another presence in the bed, and are in touch with that feeling of being whole, complete, and good as is. Later on, as you're showering, you feel the warmth of the water on your back and know in your essence that, right now, you are okay. At work, someone snaps at you and instead of reacting from a place of ego and anger, you recognize that they are suffering in some way and respond from a place of compassion. These are all moments when you touched in with your basic goodness. Tantra is simply about stringing these individual moments together to create an unbroken, continuous thread of wakefulness.

Let's look at that other term I just used: Vajrayana. *Yana,* as I noted, means "vehicle" or "path," and *vajra* means "indestructible"—this is an indestructible path. Given all the teachings the Buddha offered on everything changing all the time, what could possibly be indestructible? Your basic goodness.

When we look at the path as a cohesive whole, we realize that the innermost, secret teachings of Buddhism are all about that three-step process mentioned at the beginning of this book. We discover our true nature, that we are basically good. Having made that discovery, we strive to live a life based in basic goodness that helps everyone. The ultimate fruition of the path is that we live in a state of continuous wakefulness, being in tune with and always acting from basic goodness.

This means that everything you experience is an opportunity to contact your basic goodness. The food you eat, picking up your dog's poop, hugging a loved one, all of it. In the excellent collection of letters to and from a Zen master, Seung Sahn advises one of his students, "When you eat, only eating mind; when you drive, only driving mind."[1] When you pick up poop, only picking-up-poop mind. When you hug, only hugging mind.

All we have to do to experience basic goodness is to be present, to be here and now. Chögyam Trungpa Rinpoche coined the term "nowness" to indicate that we can be present to the very essence of this moment. If we can truly be here, now, with whatever is present, we can experience our indestructible nature.

The more we experience our own indestructible nature, the more we begin to experience the vajra nature of all things. We can interact with this present moment and see the world as it is, experiencing it as brilliant, rich, and good. The world is an expression of basic goodness and a simple, ordinary magic.

The Vajrayana path is one of relaxing entirely. It is a training of being, rather than figuring out what to be or how to act. When you hug, you shouldn't try to figure out how to hug someone. You just hug. You just be in the hug. The Vajrayana path implies that being a true meditator means trusting ourselves, specifically our basic goodness, and trusting the world and the basic goodness in it as well.

Through utilizing these three paths that the Buddha taught, and all of his many teachings, we can learn to be present and content with our lives, to be of benefit to others, to address the world as it is without laying our preconceived notions on top of it, and to playfully engage with everything that comes up in a skillful way.

The Buddhist teachings are very simple. They are about looking at our suffering and finding an end to suffering. They are a means to develop complete trust in basic goodness and to therefore live our lives fully and be of benefit to society.

A more enlightened society is possible, simply because all of us, the individuals who make up society, are already enlightened. All we have to do to achieve that society is wake up, right now, to our true nature, our basic goodness.

33 PRACTICES FOR CONNECTING WITH GOODNESS EVERYWHERE

As we near the end of our exploration of seeing goodness in society, in our environment, and, well, everywhere around us, we have to remember that the root of seeing goodness outside of ourselves begins with continually cultivating the relationship to it within ourselves. Mindfulness meditation (yes, I'm bringing it up again) forms the foundation for connecting to our own and others' basic goodness. At the same time, there are several other practices that can help us recognize this goodness as we engage with the world around us.

Post Office Meditation

While waiting in line at the post office (or the bodega, library, or anywhere else), pause for a moment. Reflect that in this moment, you and the people around you are forming a mini society. This happens to be the post office society, which is made up of the employees and customers who frequent this branch. There are certain values, such as patience and courtesy, that shape the way you relate to one another. There are also many interactions that can annoy or delight you, ranging from people you don't know holding up the line to cheerful postal workers who are simply doing their best. Pause and see if you can recognize the basic goodness in each person, even if they aren't acting in the way you would like.

Being in Nature

Wherever you live, I hope you can take some time to connect with nature. It is often very grounding for us. This could be as simple as taking off your shoes and placing your feet in the grass. In that moment, you are in open space and can just notice what arises. There might be a cool breeze, some bugs flying about, or birds chirping nearby. That itself can be an experience of basic goodness.

The Buddhist teacher Dr. Larry Ward once shared that every morning he goes to a particular tree in his yard and places his hands on it. He remarked how incredibly grounding this practice is for him. Now, you might be worried that I'm trying to get you to go hug a tree, but in this act Dr. Ward is forming a genuine connection to this living being that is older than either of us have been alive.

You might look at a tree and see just one thing, but that thing is emblematic of what we discussed about interdependence. The tree has deep roots, affecting all sorts of beings we don't even see. It creates oxygen that we don't see ourselves breathing but need to sustain our lives. Place your hands on the tree. Feel its connection to the earth beneath you and the interdependence you have with it and with this planet we share. Breathe. Relax. Feel basic goodness.

Contemplating Interdependence

When you sit down for your next meal, take a moment to reflect on how it got to you. Even a simple salad involved a network of individuals: recall that there are farmers who toiled the earth to grow the lettuce, people who harvested it, workers who transported it, employees at your local market who stocked it, and many nonhuman individuals along the way that were affected by this one salad making its way to you. The same goes for every aspect of your meal.

If you're eating at a restaurant, you can also contemplate the people who opened that establishment and those who currently work there, and realize that you are—simply by ordering a salad—part of a larger whole. You are a part of a "salad society" that exists within and outside of that restaurant. There were many, many beings who helped bring you this food so that you can be nourished and continue to do good work in this world. You can offer a moment of gratitude for them in your own words.

Drala Practice

This may sound silly, but notice the next time the environment invites you to pay attention to it. Earlier, I mentioned how children and animals often call for our attention, asking us to engage with them rather than get lost in distractions. Here I am saying that we have the same choice with nature.

There is a small tree outside my office window. Whenever I look up from my writing I see it gently swaying, and this is its invitation for me to pause, relax my gaze, and appreciate its beauty. I can experience drala every time I take a breath and simply enjoy its presence. And we know that drala does not have to be just a nature experience. It can be you walking into an art gallery where a particular piece of art catches your eye and invites you to pause and appreciate it. It can be looking out from a city rooftop and seeing a small sculpture garden on someone else's roof, when your head naturally tilts to the side and you drop whatever else you were doing and you are just *there* with it.

There are invitations like these all the time, asking us to let go of the silly thing we are preoccupied with and enter the present moment long enough to be inspired and feel uplifted.

A Practice for When You're Feeling Overwhelmed

Thus far these practices have been very pleasant: what to do when you're in nature or appreciating beauty and good food. What about when you just read the morning news and are feeling totally overwhelmed by your experience of the world?

First off, let's remember that overwhelm helps no one. It doesn't help you and won't help the people you read about in the news. Not a single civil rights leader or spiritual leader has ever said, "I was freaking out, so I just curled up in a ball, let myself remain overwhelmed, and thus made a difference in the world around me." If we want to help ourselves and others, we have to reflect not just on the suffering of the world but its goodness as well.

To begin this practice, do a short body scan. Then relax into a minute or two of mindfulness meditation. Once you are grounded in the present, contemplate the question, "What can I appreciate about this moment?" Notice what arises for you. It can be something simple, like that it is safe where you live or that you are loved. It could be something specific, like that you have a job that you enjoy or that the color of the flowers in your room pleases you. Once you've noted what has come up, ask the question again: "What can I appreciate about this moment?" After five minutes, let the question drop and simply notice how you feel. Most likely, you'll feel less overwhelmed, more in tune with the reality of this moment, and a deeper connection to your basic goodness. From this standpoint, you're in a better place to help others.

Accepting the Good and Bad

Equanimity is not about getting rid of the bad things that happen to us so as to feel peaceful. It's about holding our seat and remaining open-hearted in the midst of difficult circumstances. In this meditation we acknowledge some of the painful feelings we may experience when the chips are down while also recognizing some of the goodness around us. This practice, like many of the meditations in this book, can be accessed as a guided recording at lodrorinzler.com/youaregood.

Begin by taking a few minutes for mindfulness meditation. Then pause. Notice how you feel. Shift your attention from the breath to your emotional landscape. If it's helpful, you can ask yourself, "How am I feeling right now?" Notice what comes up in response to that question. You might notice anger coming up, or jealousy, or loneliness. You might feel appreciation or excitement. Whatever you notice is great. Just acknowledge it and then add the magic word "and" . . . and recognize the goodness that is present in this moment as well. For example:

"I'm feeling angry and . . . it's nice and warm in here."

"I'm feeling annoyed and . . . the sounds from down the hall remind me that there are people who care about me."

"I'm feeling overwhelmed . . . and the sound of the birds outside is calming."

Continue to notice what emotions arise for you, sit with them, and add the "and" statement. This helps us recognize the complex range of emotions we experience while simultaneously acknowledging the goodness that exists right alongside them.

Close with a few deep breaths and re-enter your day, further committed to knowing yourself and the goodness that exists in the world around you.

CONCLUSION: SEEING BLUE

Thank you for reading this book. It has been an incredible honor over the past fifteen years to write these words and know that you are on the other end, here with me. I am deeply grateful for your presence.

I also want to thank you for your bravery. The other day, a meditation student shared with me that beginning in the third century, Egyptian monks known as Desert Fathers would venture into the harshness of the desert in search of enlightenment. In discussing them with her academic mentor, he pointed out that Desert Fathers (and now Mothers) still make this journey into the desert to this day. He looked at her and said, "Reneé, as long as people are willing to go into the desert, the world will not end."

While she believes that her mentor meant these words literally, she also understood them metaphorically. The desert is a metaphor for the areas we fear. These are the parts of ourselves and the world around us that we do not want to look at, explore, and inhabit. As long as people like you are willing to confront this metaphorical desert, the world will not end. In fact, the world will likely thrive in response to that good work. Thank you for being willing to venture into your own desert.

A final thought: Did you know that the concept of "blue" didn't exist until around 4,500 years ago? If you go back to classic Greek, Hebrew, and Chinese texts, you can't find the word "blue" before then. This color blue that you and I take for granted simply didn't have a name.

Jules Davidoff, a professor of neuropsychology at London University, became interested in the Himba tribe of Namibia. A decade ago, he sat down with a large number of the Himba tribe and showed them twelve colored squares. The squares were identical green, except for one that was blue. He asked them, "Which one is different?"

The Himba, it turns out, didn't have a word for blue. In fact, when they looked at the squares, they didn't see the one that stood out. To them, all the squares looked the same.

Davidoff hypothesized that the reason you and I could see blue as clear as day and the Himba universally could not is that we had been introduced to blue as a color. At some point someone took you and me aside and said, "See that sky up there? It's blue." Then, once we had a category called "blue," we could see it everywhere—in clothes, furniture, on walls, and so on. But before we had a word for it, blue simply wasn't visible to us. Someone had to point it out.

The concept of basic goodness was introduced to me when I was quite young. I am fortunate in that way. My parents didn't come up with it. Nor did their spiritual teachers or even the Buddha himself. Like the color blue, this experience of our inherent goodness has existed for as long as there have been people. Yet the fact that someone pointed it out to me meant that I have had the good fortune of recognizing it in myself and others for the last several decades.

The Tibetan Buddhist teacher Chögyam Trungpa Rinpoche came up with the specific term "basic goodness" in the early 1970s. It can be translated from the Tibetan *döné sangwa*, but those two words together don't actually appear in well-known texts of Tibetan Buddhism. Trungpa Rinpoche looked at all the descriptors we have of our buddha nature and likely thought, "You know what words these Westerners might get as a way to describe their true nature? Basic goodness." And so the phrase "basic goodness" became a tool to express something timeless and universal.

These days, I see many Buddhist teachers use Trungpa Rinpoche's term, whether they are Insight teachers or Zen teachers or something else entirely. It's a good term that describes how foundational our wholeness, enoughness, or okayness truly is.

It is my sincere hope that this book will help you see your own basic goodness and that you now will see basic goodness wherever you go. When you were young and someone pointed out that the sky is blue, you began to see blue in flowers, art, and everywhere. Similarly, by introducing this experience of basic goodness, my goal is simply to have you begin to see your true nature now and increasingly more and more in the world around you.

We began this journey with an exploration of our own basic goodness, then we expanded that recognition to the people we like, dislike, and ignore. Then we looked at the world around us and said, "Huh. There's basic goodness everywhere, isn't there?"

I have been trying to point out basic goodness to people for twenty years. It would be nice to live another few decades to continue that work, but I know that may not come to be; death comes without warning, after all. In either case, at least there is now this book. If but one person reads it and discovers their true nature, deepens their relationship with it, and begins to see the world through the lens of basic goodness, then I will have done my job.

I hope that you are that person. In case no one has ever told you before, let me be the first: you are basically good. You are whole, complete, and enough as you are. Underneath the clay of your own neurosis is a golden buddha, ready to shine forth.

Okay. I'm done now. I implore you to meditate and discover these simple truths for yourself. It's one thing for someone to say, "Hey! See that? That's blue." It's another for you to then say, "Time for me to go into the world and see all the blue that I can see."

May precious basic goodness

Be discovered in those for whom it has not arisen,

And for those in whom it has been discovered,

May its presence not decline but ever increase.

ACKNOWLEDGMENTS

I'd like to thank my parents, Beth and Carl Rinzler, for raising me in a culture of basic goodness. This book would not be possible without that incredible gift.

To my wife, Adreanna Limbach—thank you for continuing to show up and love me, recognizing my basic goodness day after day, year after year. I hope we have many more decades to go together. I couldn't ask for a better partner in life and writing.

To my daughter, Ruby Rinzler—you are relentlessly present, refusing to let me live anywhere but the here and now. I'm so lucky to have you as my daughter. Every day, you inspire me.

To my teacher, Dza Kilung Rinpoche—thank you for pointing me toward my buddha nature, and for your continued guidance, wisdom, and utmost kindness.

The entire team at Shambhala Publications has been so wonderful to me over these many years. I'm deeply grateful to everyone there—and especially to Beth Frankl, who championed this project and edited it with great care.

To Stephanie Tade, my agent, who continues to go to bat for me after all these years—thank you. I could not ask for a better advocate.

To all of my friends who never give up on my basic goodness—thank you. Every day I wake up grateful to know you.

And finally, to The Basic Goodness Collective—I am honored to do this life-changing, society-changing work alongside you. Thank you for everything.

APPENDIX

Lodro currently runs a community of meditation practitioners online known as The Basic Goodness Collective. You are invited to join at lodrorinzler.com.

Our Mission Statement

We believe that all beings are basically good.

"Basic" means goodness is foundational to who we are: we are fundamentally, inherently good. Good is not "good versus evil" but a sense of being whole, complete, and enough as is.

As individuals, we seek to recognize our basic goodness and deepen our relationship with it more each day.

We know that at times we will feel disconnected to basic goodness and fall into the trap of doubt, acting in ways that are unskillful and harmful to ourselves and others. Knowing that mistakes are a part of the spiritual path, we vow to learn from them and do better day after day.

We seek to recognize the basic goodness in our families, friends, and other people we like; in the strangers we see on the street and in the news; and even in those individuals that we find difficult. Ours is a path of seeking to understand, rather than condemn, others, knowing that people do not create harm when acting from a place of basic goodness but instead do so from their own suffering. Knowing that all beings are suffering, we commit to being kind to them.

We seek to recognize the basic goodness of society. We know that society is made up of us, the people we like, the people we don't know, and the people we find difficult. Knowing that all of us possess basic goodness, we vow to try and understand the goodness that is existent within society overall.

May our work through meditation practice and study further wake us up to our true nature, and may we be of benefit to all beings.

NOTES

6. Basic Goodness Isn't Buddhist

1. "Life of the Buddha," BuddhaNet, accessed May 5, 2025, www.buddhanet.net/e-learning/buddhism /lifebuddha/18lbud/.

10. Working with Guilt and Shame

1. Pema Chödrön, *Becoming Bodhisattvas: A Guidebook for Compassionate Action* (Shambhala Publications, 2018), 120.
2. Pema Chödrön, 120.

11. Practices for Connecting with Your Basic Goodness

1. Chögyam Trungpa quoted in Andrew Holecek, *Preparing to Die: Practical Advice and Spiritual Wisdom from the Tibetan Buddhist Tradition* (Snow Lion, 2013), 22.

12. Realizing the Goodness of Others

1. Tara Brach, *Trusting the Gold: Uncovering Your Natural Goodness* (Sounds True, 2021), 1.

13. Awakening to Bodhichitta

1. Chögyam Trungpa, *Shambhala: The Sacred Path of the Warrior* (Shambhala Publications, 1984), 65.

15. Your Spouse Is Basically Good

1. Thich Nhat Hanh, "True Presence," *The Mindfulness Bell*, no. 15 (December 1995), www.parallax.org/mindfulnessbell/article/dharma-talk-true-presence-2.
2. Thich Nhat Hanh, "True Presence."

19. The Danger of Villainization

1. *On Being with Krista Tippett*, "John Lewis: Love in Action," March 28, 2013, https://onbeing.org/programs/john-lewis-love-in-action-jan2017.

20. The Two Wings of a Bird

1. "Monks in Our Midst: Thich Nhat Hanh on Understanding and Love," Monasteries of the Heart, accessed May 5, 2025, www.monasteriesoftheheart.org/blogs/monks-our-midst/thich-nhat-hanh-understanding-and-love.
2. Chögyam Trungpa, *Smile at Fear: Awakening the True Heart of Bravery* (Shambhala Publications, 2009), 9.

21. Rejoicing in Joy

1. Thich Nhat Hanh, *Being Peace* (Parallax Press, 2005), 3.

23. Society Isn't Fucked Up

1. Traleg Rinpoche, *The Essence of Buddhism* (Shambhala Publications, 2001), 13.

25. Basic Goodness in Nature

1. Chögyam Trungpa, *Shambhala: The Sacred Path of the Warrior* (Shambhala Publications, 2015), 8.

26. Drala

1. Dza Kilung Rinpoche, *The Relaxed Mind: A Seven-Step Method for Deepening Meditation Practice* (Shambhala Publications, 2015), 97.

27. There Is a Cloud Floating in This Sheet of Paper

1. Thich Nhat Hanh, *Awakening of the Heart: Essential Buddhist Sutras and Commentaries* (Parallax Press, 2012), 290.
2. Thich Nhat Hanh, *Awakening of the Heart*, 413.
3. His Holiness the Seventeenth Gyalwang Karmapa, Ogyen Trinley Dorje, "Understanding Emptiness and Interdependence," *Lion's Roar*, May 5, 2013, www.lionsroar.com/understanding-emptiness-interdependence/.

28. Basic Goodness in the News

1. Dr. Larry Ward, *Beyond the News* (podcast), accessed May 5, 2025, https://open.spotify.com/show/676ZE8AOescuYnEahIbapp.

29. Boundless Love

1. Thich Nhat Hanh, "Mara and the Buddha—Embracing Our Suffering," Plum Village, August 4, 2013, https://plumvillage.org/transcriptions/mara-and-the-buddha-embracing-our-suffering.
2. Thich Nhat Hanh, "Mara and the Buddha."

30. Basic Goodness Is Bigger Than Society

1. Dza Kilung Rinpoche, *The Relaxed Mind: A Seven-Step Method for Deepening Meditation Practice* (Shambhala Publications, 2015), 93.
2. Chögyam Trungpa, *Shambhala: The Sacred Path of the Warrior* (Shambhala Publications, 2015), 9.

31. Living a Life Without Regret

1. Bronnie Ware, "Regrets of the Dying," accessed May 5, 2025, https://bronnieware.com/blog/regrets-of-the-dying/.

32. Enlightened Society Is Right Now

1. Seung Sahn, *Only Don't Know: Selected Teaching Letters of Zen Master Seung Sahn* (Shambhala Publications, 1982), 98

Also by Lodro Rinzler

The Buddha Walks into a Bar . . .

The Buddha Walks into the Office

Love Hurts

Sit Like a Buddha

Walk Like a Buddha